Copyright

Copyright © 2026 by Ronald Jones
All rights reserved.
Published by Jones Innovative Publishing
A division of Jones Innovative Reality, LLC
Florida, US
No part of this book may be reproduced, stored in a retrieval system, or transmitted in any form or by any means, electronic, mechanical, photocopying, recording, or otherwise, without prior written permission of the publisher, except for brief quotations used in reviews, articles, or scholarly works.
This book is based on the author's personal experiences, reflections, and opinions. It is intended for informational and inspirational purposes only. It does not constitute professional, legal, medical, or financial advice. Readers are encouraged to seek appropriate professional counsel when necessary.
ISBN (Paperback): 979-8-9932273-0-6
ISBN (EPUB): 979-8-9932273-1-3
LCCN: 2025920568
First Edition
Printed in the United States of America

Preface

This book exists because too many people are being asked to heal, build, and lead without ever being shown the structure beneath the struggle.
We are told to work harder, think positively, remain disciplined, and take responsibility, often without any honest accounting of the forces shaping outcomes, the history shaping behavior, or the conditioning shaping judgment. When progress stalls, responsibility is redirected toward character instead of context, and persistence is scrutinized instead of structural design.
This book challenges that framing.
Seeds in the Soil offers a structural examination of how mindset, history, power, and conditioning intersect, and how clarity, discipline, and alignment produce durable change. It is written to challenge assumptions, slow thinking, and replace reaction with intention.
This book assumes you are capable of responsibility.
It does not ask you to be perfect. It asks you to be honest.
Each chapter builds on the one before it. Skipping sections may feel efficient, but it weakens the outcome. The ideas here are meant to be applied, not merely understood. Read slowly. Pause when something unsettles you. Discomfort is not a signal to reject what you are reading; it is often a signal that something real has been touched.
These pages will challenge how you understand yourself, your history, and the patterns you've inherited. That challenge is intentional. Growth does not emerge from reassurance. It emerges from clarity.
This book does not ask for agreement. It asks for examination.
If you are looking for validation, reassurance, or simple answers, this book may frustrate you. If you are willing to think systemically, reflect honestly, and take responsibility for what you can control, it will serve you well.
This is not a book about blame.
It is a book about capacity.
Capacity to see clearly.
Capacity to choose deliberately.
Capacity to build something that lasts.
What follows is not theory for theory's sake. It is a framework for understanding why the ground looks the way it does and how different seeds produce different outcomes.
Read with intention. Apply with discipline.
And remember, growth begins beneath the surface, long before it becomes visible.

The UPROOT Method

UPROOT is the framework that guides this entire book.
It is not a slogan. It is a process. Each stage builds on the one before it.
Skipping steps weakens outcomes.

U — *Understand the Soil*
Growth does not begin with action. It begins with assessment. This stage examines the conditions, beliefs, histories, incentives, and underlying structures that shaped current outcomes. Nothing forms in a vacuum. Understanding the soil means recognizing what was inherited, what was normalized, and what forces shaped your position before you ever made a choice.

P — *Pull the Weeds*
Not everything in the soil belongs there. This stage removes inherited lies, destructive habits, psychological traps that drain energy and distort decision-making. Left unaddressed, they consume resources meant for growth.

R — *Restore the Roots*
Growth requires stability. This stage focuses on repairing what anchors life: identity, trust, health, emotional regulation, and internal coherence. Without strong roots, progress collapses under pressure. Restoration is not cosmetic. It is foundational.

O — *Organize the Ground*
Growth without structure is fragile. This stage introduces coordination, discipline, and alignment beyond individual action. Organization turns intention into capacity and movement into leverage. What is not organized cannot scale.

O — *Own the Process*
Ownership is responsibility. This stage moves beyond participation into authority, building enterprises and institutions that function without constant supervision. Control requires designing what can endure beyond personal effort. What you do not own, you eventually lose influence over.

T — *Transfer the Harvest*
Nothing matters if it dies with you. This stage ensures continuity through protection, documentation, teaching, and succession. What is built must be guarded, understood, and intentionally passed forward.

UPROOT is not linear once completed. It is cyclical.
Each generation returns to the soil, removes newly grown weeds, restores damaged roots, organizes structures, claims responsibility, and transfers what was built forward.
This method is not theoretical. It is applied throughout every chapter. The work begins now.

PART 1 — The Soil: Breaking Mental Ground

Chapter 1 – Stolen Focus
How They Keep Us Running in Place

Are you exhausted?
Not just tired, but worn down by work, bills, and the constant pressure of life.
Do most days feel like a Monday?
Rushing to get ready. Sitting in traffic. Clocking in. Dealing with workplace politics, unrealistic expectations, and the quiet frustration of knowing you are giving your best energy to something that barely gives back.
Before the day even starts, the tone is set.
News headlines feed anxiety. Messages demand responses. Family needs attention. Relationships require maintenance. Social media fills every pause.
By the time the day is over, you are drained but not fulfilled.
Busy, but not advancing.
Occupied, but not positioned.
That exhaustion is often blamed on laziness, lack of discipline, or not wanting it badly enough.
That explanation is wrong.
What most people are experiencing is not failure.
It is fragmented attention.
This book is not competing with other books.
It is competing with your phone, your fatigue, your stress, your responsibilities, and a system that benefits when you are too busy surviving to sit still long enough to think.   This book will ask you to slow down, not because you are behind, but because clarity requires space. Focus is not a personality trait.
It is a resource.
And like every valuable resource, it has always been targeted.
Most people assume distraction is a modern inconvenience. Phones, notifications, noise, and entertainment. That explanation is shallow.
Distraction is not accidental, and it is not neutral. It is functional.
Distraction keeps populations reactive, consumption-focused, and depleted, ensuring their energy is spent without threatening the incentives that depend on it. The first thing taken from any people is not land.
It is attention.
Because attention determines what you notice, what you question, and what you tolerate. When focus is fractured, agency collapses quietly. People stay busy, not powerful. Moving, not advancing. Occupied, not positioned.
This chapter begins where most conversations avoid. Not with money. Not with politics. But with the mind's ability to stay oriented long enough to think.

Distraction Is a Strategy, not a Flaw

Modern economic and cultural systems do not block ambition.
They absorb it and quietly redirect it.
They keep people busy, stressed, and distracted just enough to prevent them from asking the most important question:

Who benefits from the way my life is structured?

A distracted mind is easy to manage.
It jumps from issue to issue without resolving any of them. It mistakes urgency for importance. It confuses motion with progress. It burns energy responding to stimuli instead of directing action toward outcomes.
It is conditioning.
From early education to modern media, attention has been trained to fragment. Shortened time horizons. Constant interruption. Reward loops that favor reaction over reflection. None of this required force. Incentives were enough.
When people cannot hold focus, they cannot build structure.
When they cannot build structure, they remain dependent on what others control.

Why Focus Comes Before Everything Else

You cannot repair what you cannot observe.
You cannot plan what you cannot hold in mind.
You cannot organize what you cannot concentrate on long enough to understand.
Focus is the gateway skill. Every other capacity, discipline, strategy, financial literacy, health, and leadership depends on sustained attention.
This is why stolen focus is always the first loss and the last one addressed.
A distracted person may work harder than anyone in the room and still produce nothing that compounds. Effort without focus dissipates. Energy leaks everywhere.

Busyness Is Not Productivity

Busyness is often praised as a virtue.
In reality, it is frequently avoidance.
When attention is scattered, people stay occupied with tasks that feel urgent but change nothing. Meetings without decisions. Conversations without outcomes. Consumption without creation.
Busyness keeps people exhausted enough to avoid asking harder questions:
- Why does nothing feel stable?
- Why does progress reset?

- Why does exertion never seem to compound?

The answer is not laziness.
It is misdirected attention.

Visibility Is Not Power

The system does not fear visible success.
It fears independent power.
Everywhere you look, you see Black success. Athletes, entertainers, influencers, and a small circle of billionaires. Their faces fill screens so consistently that success begins to feel common, even expected.
Quietly, a belief settles in.
If they made it, the system must be fair.
But visibility is not power.
Representation is not control.
Money without ownership still answers to rules written elsewhere. A few winners do not mean the game is open. They make it look open. And that illusion stabilizes belief in the system itself.
Watch what happens when a Black celebrity, athlete, or billionaire steps outside the approved lane. Questions narratives. Challenges institutions. Threatens economic interests. Access closes. Endorsements disappear. Platforms turn hostile. Then comes the correction.
The message is never subtle.
This is where the line is.
Success inside a system is not control of the system.

Checkers in a Chess World

On the surface, the board looks equal.
Same laws. Same money. Same country.
But equality of appearance is not equality of function.
Some people were trained to play chess.
Long horizons. Delayed gratification. Positional thinking. Frameworks designed to outlast individuals.
Others were trained to play checkers.
Fast movement. Immediate reaction. Survival under pressure. Every move responds to what is already happening.
These are not differences in intelligence.
There are differences in training.
Chess rewards patience.
Checkers rewards speed.
One builds power.
The other survives instability.

The Attention Economy

Control no longer requires force.
It requires saturation.
Where power once extracted labor from bodies, it now extracts value from attention. Endless headlines. Outrage cycles. Celebrity collapse. Political spectacle. Constant reaction.
People feel informed without gaining control.
Engaged without being empowered.
Outrage replaces strategy.
Entertainment replaces education.
Debate replaces construction.
The system does not require ignorance.
It requires constant stimulation.

Conditioned, Not Broken

Not about intelligence.
Not laziness.
Not lack of ambition.
Brilliance has always existed. But brilliance buried in poor soil struggles to grow.
When distraction becomes constant, depth feels uncomfortable. Stillness feels unnatural. Focus feels foreign. People stay busy without building, informed without direction, connected without organizing.
Failure was not chosen.
No one taught us to protect the soil before demanding the harvest.

The First Commitment

Before pulling weeds, before restoring roots, before building anything, attention must be reclaimed.
This chapter asks only one thing:
Pay attention to where your focus goes without permission.
Notice what pulls you into reaction.
Notice what fragments your time.
Notice what keeps you busy but not advancing.
Do not judge it yet.
Just observe.
Understanding the soil begins with noticing what has been planted in your mind and who benefits from it remaining there.

What Comes Next

Once the battlefield is established, the next question is not how hard people push, but how power, incentives, and structure shape outcomes.
It is intentionality.
Growth Was Not Accidental
It is about what was planted.
Chapter 2: The Weed They Planted examines how harmful beliefs were introduced, reinforced, and protected, often so early and so consistently that they came to feel natural.
You cannot remove weeds that you believe grew on their own.
And you cannot heal what you refuse to examine.
Before anything can be uprooted, the origin must be understood.
The next chapter is where that work begins.

Chapter 2 – The Unseen Script
What Was Planted on Purpose

Seeing Ourselves Through Borrowed Eyes

"You have to decide who you are and force the world to deal with you, not with its idea of you." James Baldwin

Nothing harmful survives this long by accident.
Beliefs do not move across generations without reinforcement.
Behaviors do not repeat for centuries without incentive.
Outcomes do not remain predictable without design.
When the same patterns appear across time, environments, and personalities, randomness is no longer a reasonable explanation.
What remains is structure.
This chapter is about the difference between what grew naturally and what was planted intentionally.
Most people are taught to think of beliefs as personal opinions. In reality, beliefs are often inherited habits of thought. They shape what feels possible, what feels risky, what feels normal, and what feels unrealistic long before conscious choice ever enters the picture.
You do not choose most of your assumptions.
You absorb them.
The most effective forms of control do not announce themselves as control.
They present themselves as common sense.

Conditioning Works Best When It Feels Familiar

If harmful beliefs arrived as obvious lies, they would be rejected. If exploitation arrived as open hostility, it would be resisted. So, neither arrives that way.
They arrive as:
• Advice
• Tradition
• Humor
• Survival wisdom
• Cultural norms
• Repeated stories about who succeeds and why
Over time, repetition replaces examination. What is familiar feels true.
What is common feels inevitable.
This is how people begin defending arrangements that drain them, not out of loyalty, but because those arrangements start to feel like reality itself.

The Script Was Never About Inferiority

One of the most persistent misunderstandings is the idea that harmful conditioning was designed to convince people they were inferior. That is too simple.
The deeper goal was to limit range.
You do not need people to believe they are worthless. You only need them to believe certain outcomes are unrealistic, dangerous, or not for them. You only need them to self-edit before they reach the edge of possibility.
The most effective barriers live inside expectation.
If someone believes ownership is risky, leadership is rare, coordination is dangerous, and long-term planning is unrealistic, they will stay within approved lanes without enforcement.
That is how freedom is limited quietly.

Beliefs Are the Most Portable Control Mechanism

Laws require enforcement.
Violence requires visibility.
Beliefs require neither.
Once beliefs are internalized, control no longer has to be enforced. People pull themselves back. They explain away barriers. They normalize instability. They rationalize imbalance.
They say things like:
- That's just how it is
- It's always been like this
- Be grateful for what you have
- Don't rock the boat
- Focus on yourself
- Mind your business

Each phrase sounds harmless.
Each one discourages coordination.
Each one preserves the status quo.

How the Script Was Reinforced

The script was not taught once. It was reinforced everywhere.
Education-trained compliance before curiosity.
Media rewarded visibility over ownership.
Workplaces rewarded loyalty over leverage.
Religion was often stripped of liberation and reframed as endurance.
Success stories were framed as rare exceptions instead of repeatable paths.
When people did succeed, the narrative focused on talent, hustle, or luck.
Rarely on structure, coordination, or institutional support.
This was not accidental storytelling.

It was risk management.
Control is preserved when success is framed as personal rather than reproducible.
They are threatened by groups who understand it is structural.

Why Survival Wisdom Became a Trap

Many inherited beliefs were once adaptive. Silence reduced danger. Obedience reduced punishment. Staying small, reduced visibility. Survival-focused thinking reduced immediate harm while trading away long-term power.
Those strategies kept people alive.
But strategies that preserve life under threat often limit growth when the environment changes. When survival wisdom is passed down without revision, it becomes a ceiling disguised as protection.
What once protected bodies can now restrict futures.
This is why questioning inherited beliefs can feel like betrayal. You are not just challenging ideas. You are challenging strategies that once kept people safe.
That discomfort is real.
It is also necessary.

The Difference Between Culture and Conditioning

Culture is chosen and adaptive.
Conditioning is imposed and rigid.
Culture evolves when conditions change.
Conditioning resists change even when it causes harm.
If a belief cannot be questioned without guilt, fear, or shame, it is likely conditioning, not culture.
If a belief consistently benefits people outside your community more than those within it, it deserves examination.

The Cost of Unexamined Scripts

When beliefs go unexamined:
- Ownership feels unrealistic
- Coordination feels dangerous
- Planning feels indulgent
- Power feels inaccessible
- Rest feels irresponsible
- Boundaries feel selfish

People work hard, stay busy, and remain stuck.
Not because they lack commitment.

Because their energy is being applied inside a framework designed to absorb it.

Seeing the Script Is the First Break

You cannot remove what you cannot name.
This chapter does not ask you to reject everything you were taught.
It asks you to distinguish between wisdom and limitation, between protection and control, between culture and conditioning.
Some beliefs still serve you.
Others have expired.
Clarity begins when you stop asking whether a belief feels familiar and start asking who benefits from it remaining unquestioned.

Where This Leaves Us

In Chapter 1, we reclaimed focus.
In this chapter, we identified what that focus was trained to overlook.
Once you see the script, you cannot unsee it.
And once you see it, the next step becomes unavoidable.
Noticing is not enough.
Removal is required.
Chapter 3 examines how these scripts shape identity, stress, health, and behavior at the psychological level. Because beliefs do not live only in thought.
They live in the body.
The weeds were planted.
Now we examine what they do below the surface.

Chapter 3 – The Psychology of Racism
The Programming of Pain

Racism survives not because of hatred alone, but because it learned how to reproduce.
It no longer depends on open hostility.
It moves through narratives, institutions, habits, and expectations we were trained to absorb long before we had language for them.
You already know racism exists.
What most of us were never taught is how it keeps working.
Not just between groups, but inside us.
Not only through laws or visible conflict, but through repetition, permission, and normalization.
Not only as something we respond to, but as something many of us were trained to live inside.
This chapter examines why racism continues, how it adapts across generations, and how it quietly shapes behavior, stress responses, identity, and self-perception, even when we consciously reject it.
Because lasting dominance is sustained through habits, incentives, and beliefs, not brute pressure.
They rely on psychology.

Racism Is Not a Feeling. It Is a Program. It is Operational

Racism is often explained as hatred, but that explanation is simple; it misses the mechanism.
Hatred is emotional.
Racism is operational.
Feelings flare and fade. Programs persist.
Racism survives because it does not require constant hostility. It runs whether people are angry or calm, conscious of it or not. It operates like software, installed through repetition, reinforced by authority, and normalized through everyday life.
Think about how software updates work.
You do not design them.
You do not vote on them.
You do not even read most of what they change.
They are pushed out, downloaded automatically, and suddenly your phone behaves a little differently. Not because you chose it, but because the system requires it to keep operating.
Racial narratives work the same way.
Stories get pushed.
Images repeat.
Certain groups are framed as problems to manage, while others are framed as defaults to protect.

Over time, those updates stop feeling like updates. They start feeling like reality.
That is how racism stays alive without anyone needing to announce it.

The Body Learns Before the Mind

Racism does not begin with belief.
It begins with the nervous system.
Long before we argue about fairness or intent, the body learns patterns:
- Where caution is rewarded
- Where silence feels safer
- Where being seen too clearly comes with consequences

What looks like weakness was survival under pressure.
The nervous system's job is not justice. It is protection.
So when you walk into certain spaces and feel watched, not tense, not panicked, just aware, that awareness did not come from nowhere.
The nervousness does not end at the register.
You still have to walk through the anti-theft sensors, holding your breath, hoping the cashier removed every tag, hoping there will not be that sound, the one that turns you into a spectacle for doing nothing wrong.
And when you hesitate before relaxing, before speaking freely, before trusting how you will be received, that hesitation was learned.
Not taught in a lesson.
Taught through outcomes.
The body reacts first. The story that explains it comes later.
That is how racism operates without ever announcing itself.

When Harm Is Made Normal

There is a reason these patterns live in the body. They were formed in environments where Black life was publicly violated, witnessed, and normalized without consequence.
When harm is repeated and unpunished, the body learns before the mind has a chance to object.
This history does not live only in photographs, textbooks, or documentaries. It settles into posture, vigilance, restraint, and the quiet calculations people make about where it is safe to exist fully.
Individual blame misses the issue. The real question is how structures trained entire populations to accept, excuse, or ignore harm.
Dehumanization does not require cruelty to be effective. It only requires repetition, authority, and time.
When something is made ordinary long enough, empathy does not disappear violently. It fades quietly.
That fading has consequences for everyone.

What Fades and Why It Matters

When harm is made ordinary, something essential begins to fade.
Not memory.
Not history.
Not pain.
What fades is the felt connection.
Empathy does not disappear all at once. It thins. It dulls. It becomes selective. And that fading reshapes everyone it touches.
For those who benefit from the system, empathy fades into abstraction. Suffering becomes something understood intellectually but not carried emotionally. It becomes history, policy, debate, or unfortunate circumstance, something to be explained rather than felt.
This allows life to continue without reckoning. It protects identity and comfort, but it comes at a cost. When empathy fades, moral clarity weakens. The capacity to sit with discomfort erodes. The relationship becomes defensive. Humanity becomes conditional.
For those who carry the cost of the system, something else fades. Not awareness. Not vigilance. Not memory.
What fades is expectation.
Expectation that harm will be acknowledged.
Expectation that empathy will show up.
Expectation that dignity will be protected without negotiation.
Over time, that fading hardens into posture. Into restraint. Into self-policing. Into emotional armor that looks like strength but is really survival.
Neither fading is healing.
One side learns not to feel too much.
The other learns not to hope too much.
And when that happens, harm does not end. It simply moves. It relocates from public outrage into private bodies, behaviors, and inherited silence.
This is why the consequences are collective.
A society cannot remain healthy when one group is trained to numb, and another is trained to brace. When empathy fades on one side, and trust fades on the other, the connection collapses. Fear fills the gap. People talk past one another. Order is maintained on the surface while pressure accumulates underneath.
Healing does not require forgetting.
It requires precision.
Black people are not being asked to let pain fade. Pain carries information. Memory carries truth. What must fade is the belief that recognition must come before agency, that survival responses define identity, or that healing must wait on permission.
Those who benefit from the system are not being asked to accept guilt. They are being asked to recover feeling, to interrupt numbness, to rehumanize what abstraction erased, and to choose honesty over comfort.
When what fades is named, it can be reclaimed.

When empathy is restored to feeling and expectation is restored to dignity, healing becomes possible, not by denial, but by choice.

Scar Story: Educated Into Chains

In the fifth grade, I learned something about America that no textbook ever explained directly.
Our teacher assigned *The Adventures of Tom Sawyer* and *The Adventures of Huckleberry Finn*. Each day, students were called on to read aloud from their desks, page by page, in order. This was framed as education. This was the curriculum.
I was the only Black child in the room.
The first time we reached the word **nigger**, the room changed.
The student paused. You could see the unease on his face, the recognition that this was a word he had been taught not to say, a word he had also been taught was connected to me. He glanced in my direction. Then he looked at the teacher.
The teacher's eyes were flat. Unbothered.
She gave a small nod. The kind that says, go ahead, it's fine.
And then the word came out.
Out loud.
Clear.
Normal.
It was not my name. But it landed in my body like it was.
At first, the room felt awkward. Heavy. You could hear a pin drop.
Everyone seemed aware that something had shifted, even if they did not know how to name it.
I sat there wondering not just how the word felt, but why this book was being taught at all. What were we supposed to learn from it? What lesson did the education system believe this was delivering, and to whom?
That question stayed with me.
Because I was already learning a different lesson outside the classroom.
Before Utah, I lived in Baltimore, Maryland. Majority Black. Familiar. Grounded. I had never experienced racism as something directed at me in a sustained way. Utah was different. Everything was new. We were visibly out of place.
When I was with my stepmother, there were moments when people said things, jokes, comments, and remarks meant to remind us that we were not part of the neighborhood. Watermelon jokes. Side remarks. Laughter that lingered too long.
Each time, I would feel something rise in me.
And each time, my stepmother would quietly say, "Ignore it. Do not give them what they want. Just keep moving."
That was the script.
Not because she was weak.
Because she understood escalation.

Because she understood cost.
So, by the time I sat in that classroom, I already knew how to respond.
Do not react.
Do not disrupt.
Stay quiet and let it pass.
What made the classroom experience worse was how quickly the discomfort disappeared.
By the end of the week, there was no more hesitation. No more glances.
Students read the word without looking up. The room was quiet, not tense, just settled.
Repetition had done what repetition always does. It made the unacceptable feel ordinary.
That is when I understood something I did not have language for yet. The word was not just being read. It was being authorized. The system had decided my presence did not require protection. My reaction did not matter. The lesson would continue with or without me.
I did not go home and protest.
I did not explode.
I endured.
At the time, that felt mature. Practical. Smart.
Only later did I understand what had really happened.
That classroom was not just teaching literature.
It was a teaching hierarchy.
It was teaching silence.
It was teaching me how to live beneath a story that was not written for me.
I am now in my fifties, and I can still remember that week with clarity.
That is not because I am holding onto pain.
It is because my body learned something it was never meant to forget.
It was not the word. It was permission.

Why Context Changes Everything

Here is the question that matters:
Would I have felt anything at all if that classroom had been filled with Black students and a Black teacher?
Probably not.
Same word.
Same book.
Completely different outcome.
Because the issue was never just the word.
It was permission.
It was authority.
It was who controlled the space.
When authority allows harm and calls it education, the lesson goes deeper than content. It teaches who is protected and who is expendable.

That difference explains why the same experience can feel harmless in one environment and traumatic in another.
And it exposes the system underneath.

Internalized Racism Is Not Self-Hatred. It Is Training

Internalized racism did not begin as hostility toward ourselves or each other. It emerged as a survival adaptation. When safety is tied to proximity to power, people learn to adjust.
When silence reduces risk, silence becomes intelligence.
When correction comes faster from inside the group than outside it, people learn to police one another.
That logic was learned long before we were born.
Over time, it shows up as:
- Judging other Black people more harshly than anyone else
- Mistrusting Black leadership while extending grace elsewhere
- Confusing survival behaviors with character flaws

Blame is not the lens.
It is about inheritance.
What once kept people alive can later keep them limited.

Why This Still Matters Now

Racism does not survive because people keep hating.
It survives because it keeps running.
Quietly.
Routinely.
Often without being named.
What you have seen in this chapter is not a feeling.
It is a system.
It is operational.
And because it operates beneath awareness, it often goes uninterrupted.
Seeing this does not require guilt.
It requires honesty.
If training shaped behavior, then behavior can be reshaped.
If survival responses were learned, they can be unlearned.
Awareness is not the end of the work.
It is the moment choice becomes possible.
What begins in the mind does not stay there.
It moves into the body.
Into stress.
Into posture.
Into health.
Into what gets carried forward.
Chapter 4 examines how unresolved pain becomes inheritance.

Not as blame, but as transmission.
Because what is not processed does not disappear.
It passes.

Chapter 4 – Inherited Pain
How Trauma Became Inheritance

Many of the reactions we carry feel automatic. Trust can feel risky even when nothing is obviously wrong. Rest can feel uncomfortable. Peace can feel unfamiliar. These responses are often reframed as personal flaws, laziness, anger issues, commitment problems, being told "you don't know how to communicate," "you're emotionally unavailable," or "you're always on guard."

But these responses are not weakness, lack of discipline, or moral failure. They are inherited. Pain does not live only in memory; it lives in the body. Trauma is not just what happened to us, but what the nervous system learned to do to survive what happened. When danger repeats, the body adapts. It learns to stay alert, to react quickly, to trust slowly, and to treat uncertainty as a threat. That adaptation can keep a person alive in harmful conditions. But when the environment changes, or the danger ends, and the adaptation remains, survival strategies begin shaping behavior, relationships, parenting, and family life. That is how pain moves from an experience into a pattern, from a pattern into a culture, and from a culture into a legacy.

When Survival Becomes the Default

Trauma is often misunderstood because it is measured by memory instead of behavior. If you cannot recall one dramatic event, people assume nothing happened. If you cannot point to a single moment, you are expected to "move on." But trauma does not live primarily in thought. It lives in the nervous system.

Trauma is not only what happened. It is what your body learned to do to survive what happened. When pressure is constant, the nervous system adjusts. It becomes faster to react, slower to trust, more sensitive to disrespect, less tolerant of uncertainty, always scanning for what could go wrong. That is not dysfunction. That is intelligence under pressure.

The cost comes when that survival wiring becomes the default setting. You stay guarded even when love is offered. You stay busy even when rest is available. You stay braced even when life is calm. What once protected you begins to restrict you. What once kept you safe starts narrowing your life.

Pain Becomes Culture When It Goes Unspoken

Trauma does not need language to transfer. Children do not learn the world through explanations. They learn it through exposure. Before a child understands words, they absorb tone. Before they can explain behavior, they study reactions. Before they know the rules, they feel consequences. Learning happens long before instruction begins.

A parent does not have to say, "The world is unsafe." The child feels it in the tension when you walk through the door. Fear does not need to be explained. It shows up as control, as snapping instead of listening, as hovering instead of guiding. Distrust does not need a definition. It shows up when promises are broken casually, when emotions are dismissed, when discipline depends on mood instead of principle.

Children learn through:
- Tone before words
- Behavior before explanation
- Reactions before instruction

Over time, survival behaviors are rebranded. Control gets called protection. Hypervigilance gets called love. Silence gets called strength. Emotional neglect gets called independence. Slowly, what began as a response to danger becomes tradition. "This is just how we are." "This is just how our family is." "That's just how men are." "That's just how life is."

That is how inherited pain hides in plain sight. It does not announce itself as trauma. It gets renamed to normal.

What Children Learn When They Are Not the Priority

When adults live undisciplined, inconsistent, or emotionally unavailable lives, children do not experience freedom.

They experience instability.

They learn, quietly and repeatedly:
- That attention must be earned through disruption
- That authority is unpredictable
- That love comes attached to tension

When adults live reactively, children grow up hyper-aware, not resilient. They learn to scan rooms, read emotions, and adjust themselves to survive adult behavior.

That is not maturity.

That is adaptation.

And adaptation to chaos always carries a cost.

How Neglect Gets Renamed as Normal

A parent does not have to say, "I am overwhelmed."
The child feels it when they are treated like an inconvenience.
A caregiver does not need to admit fear.
It shows up as excessive restriction or explosive discipline.
A household does not need to name instability.
Children learn it when rules shift daily, consequences are random, and accountability disappears.
Over time, survival behaviors are rebranded:
- Control gets called protection

- Hypervigilance gets called love
- Silence gets called strength
- Emotional neglect gets called independence

Slowly, what began as a response to danger becomes tradition.
"This is just how we are."
"This is just how our family is."
"That's just how men are."
"That's just how life is."
That is how inherited pain hides in plain sight.
It does not announce itself as trauma.
It gets renamed normal.

Survival Mode Has a Cost

Survival mode is effective in emergencies. It is destructive as a permanent lifestyle. When survival becomes the default, long-term planning feels unrealistic. Rest feels irresponsible. Joy feels suspicious. Stillness feels unsafe. Trust feels risky.
People stay busy. They stay alert. They stay guarded. Not because they want to, but because their body never received the signal that the danger changed.

When Calm Feels Unsafe

If you have ever sat in a quiet room and felt your mind start racing, like silence itself was threatening, that is not you being dramatic. That is your nervous system saying, *I don't recognize this calm. I don't know what to do with it.*

Why Familiar Pain Feels Like Love

One of the most damaging effects of inherited pain is confusing familiarity with safety.
When chaos is normal, peace feels boring.
When tension is familiar, calm feels foreign.
When love always came with pressure, consistency feels suspicious.
So people unconsciously choose:
- Relationships that mirror stress
- Environments that recreate pressure
- Situations that justify vigilance

This reflects conditioning and context more than character or judgment.
Often, it is nervous-system loyalty.
The body seeks what it recognizes.
That is how people become loyal to patterns that hurt them, because those patterns feel like home.

The Family Is the First Classroom

Before school.
Before media.
Before work, church, or politics.
The family teaches:
- How conflict is handled
- How emotions are expressed
- How love is shown or withheld
- How authority is approached
- What is safe to say out loud
- What must be swallowed

When families are shaped by unresolved trauma, children inherit coping, not clarity.
And coping is not the same as living.
A household can function while everyone is emotionally starving.
A family can survive while no one feels safe being fully human.

Strength Without Healing Becomes Hardness

There is a myth we were raised on: strength requires suffering.
It does not.
Strength requires capacity.
Unhealed pain often disguises itself as:
- Toughness
- Independence
- Emotional "control"
- Resilience
- "I'm good."
- "I don't need nobody."

Beneath that posture is often exhaustion.
You can survive anything and still be wounded by it.
Endurance is not freedom.

Why Unhealed Pain Remains Useful to Power

This shows up everywhere reaction is rewarded more than strategy, in workplaces, politics, relationships, and communities where constant urgency replaces long-term planning.
Unhealed people react.
Healed people organize.
Unresolved pain:
- Shortens attention
- Fuels conflict
- Erodes trust

- Fragments unity
- Makes patience feel impossible

A population operating in survival mode is easier to manage than one grounded in regulation, clarity, and discipline.
That is not paranoia.
That is pattern recognition.
If the body is exhausted, the mind cannot build strategy.
If the mind cannot build strategy, it stays trapped in cycles.
And cycles keep behavior predictable.
Healing is not just personal relief.
It is a threat to structures that rely on constant reaction.

The Truth We Avoid

Children do not inherit your intentions.
They inherit your patterns.
They do not remember what you meant.
They remember how it felt to live with you.
If pain is never named, examined, or interrupted, it does not disappear.
It gets organized into behavior.
Then into identity.
Then into culture.

Why This Chapter Exists

Parents acted within the limits of what they were taught and allowed.
Not about shaming families.
Not about denying resilience.
It is about breaking cycles.
What protected earlier generations under pressure may now be harming the next.
Love without discipline is not love.
Structure without care is not safety.
Healing begins when adults stop calling dysfunction "normal" and take responsibility for what children are learning before a word is ever spoken.

Reflection: Interrupting the Transfer

Do not perform this. Do not overthink it. Be honest.
Where do you stay on guard even when nothing is wrong?
Where does peace feel unfamiliar?
What emotions do you swallow automatically?
What patterns were called strength but felt costly?
Which behaviors helped you survive but now cost you intimacy, rest, or stability?

Ask yourself one clean question this week:
Is this me, or is this inheritance?
That question is not about shame.
It is about choice.

Where This Leaves Us

We now understand:
- How identity was distorted
- How beliefs were programmed
- How pain was inherited

But awareness alone does not repair anything.
Healing requires interruption.
Repair requires intention.
Unity requires trust.
That work comes next.

Chapter 5: Repair the Foundation

Exposure without repair leads to collapse. Before anything new is built, the foundation must be strengthened.

Chapter 5 — Repair the Foundation
Restoring the Black Family Blueprint

Every structure carries the memory of how it was built.
If the foundation is cracked, the upper floors do not matter.
You can decorate dysfunction, but you cannot build a legacy on it.
This chapter exists because no conversation about wealth, power, or leadership survives a broken foundation. And whether we like it or not, the family is the first institution every society forms. Long before banks, courts, schools, or governments, the family taught people how to live together, resolve conflict, transmit values, and prepare the next generation.
When that institution is unstable, every system downstream absorbs the cost.
Repair does not begin with money.
It begins with structure.

Understanding Before Judgment

Let this be clear.
This recognizes the weight Black mothers carried within constrained conditions.
It is not an indictment of Black fathers.
It is not nostalgia for a past that never fully existed.
But it is also not an excuse chapter.
What we are dealing with today is not random. It is not mysterious. And it is not morally neutral. Much of what we see is adaptation under pressure. But adaptations designed for crisis cannot become permanent architecture.
There is context.
And there is accountability.
Both must exist for repair to happen.

What the Family Was Designed to Do

At its core, the family was designed to transmit six things no outside institution can replace.

Identity
The family was meant to answer the first and most important question a child ever asks: Who am I? Not in theory, but in practice. Identity gives grounding before the world tries to name a child. When identity is absent at home, children search for it elsewhere, often in places designed to exploit confusion.

Values
Values are not slogans or rules posted on walls. They are demonstrated priorities. What matters. What does not. What is tolerated. What is corrected. Values teach children how to choose when no one is watching.

Protection
Protection is not control. It is safety with boundaries. It is knowing someone is paying attention, intervening early, and creating stability so a child does not have to live in constant alert.
Discipline
Discipline is not punishment. It is structure. It teaches cause and effect, patience, restraint, and responsibility. Without discipline, children grow up reacting instead of directing their lives.
Emotional Regulation
Families were meant to teach how to handle anger, disappointment, fear, and stress without collapse. Children who never learn regulation become adults who struggle to coordinate, commit, or lead under pressure.
Economic Cooperation
Before banks, families pooled resources. Before courts, families resolved conflict. Before schools, families trained character. Economic cooperation taught that survival and progress were collective, not isolated.
What follows is structure, not sentiment.
It is anthropology.
When the family functions, everything downstream stabilizes.
When it fractures, every system absorbs the cost.

How the Blueprint Was Disrupted

The disruption was intentional.
Enslavement severed lineage, naming, authority, and continuity. Men were removed or neutralized. Women were overburdened. Children were raised in instability and fear. After emancipation, the pressure did not end. It changed form.
Economic exclusion.
Criminalization.
Policies that penalized family unity.
Narratives that reframed survival as dysfunction.
What began as forced separation hardened into normalized absence, not because families lacked love, but because stability was systematically denied.

The Cost of Forced Independence

One of the most misunderstood realities in Black America is independence.
Much of what is praised as strength was never chosen. It was required.
Women learned to carry households alone.
Men learned that presence did not guarantee protection or provision.
Children learned to mature early.
Independence kept families alive.
But it came at a cost.

Strength without support leads to exhaustion.
Responsibility without reinforcement leads to resentment.
Exhaustion reshapes expectations.
Survival became the goal. Stability became optional.

When Roles Collapse

When roles are unclear, people compete instead of cooperating.
Children become observers instead of participants.
Leadership turns reactive instead of intentional.
Love may exist, but structure does not.
The instability feels personal.
But it is structural.

Masculinity Without Chains

This must be said carefully and clearly.
Masculinity is not domination.
It is stabilization.
At its healthiest, masculine leadership provides presence, protection, provision, restraint, and accountability. When men are absent, physically or emotionally, relational capacity collapses. But presence alone is not enough. Leadership requires emotional regulation, discipline, foresight, and responsibility beyond self.
Men are not saviors.
They are stabilizers.
And stabilization is learned.

The Silent Weight on Black Women

Black women did not become strong because strength was glamorous.
They became strong because weakness was punished.
For generations, Black women carried households, emotions, children, and trauma at the same time. They were expected to survive without softness, lead without rest, and nurture without being nurtured.
Exhaustion got mislabeled as independence.
Self-sacrifice got praised as a virtue.
Asking for help began to feel unsafe.
Empowerment without structure collapses.
It is survival extended too long.
Black women were never the problem.
They were the backbone.
Healing does not require stronger shoulders.
It requires a shared load.

The Silent Drift of Black Men

Black men did not become distant because they did not care.
Presence was punished long before absence was chosen. Many were never shown stabilized leadership, only reaction and defense. Manhood was assembled from fragments.
Peers instead of mentors.
Chaos instead of continuity.
Reaction instead of intention.
Confusion hardened into posture.
Accountability felt like an attack.
Partnership felt like a loss of control.
The purpose here is understanding, not accusation.
It is a diagnosis.
At some point, survival stops being an explanation and becomes a choice.
Children do not need perfect fathers.
They need present ones.
Women do not need saviors.
They need partners.
Accountability is not punishment.
It is power reclaimed.

Children Learn What They Watch

Children do not listen to lectures.
They study patterns.
How conflict is handled.
How love is expressed.
How authority behaves.
How stress is managed.
The family is not only emotional.
It is instructional.
Children do not inherit intentions.
They inherit patterns.

Repair Is Not Reversal

We are not going backward.
We are not recreating the past.
We are repairing with intention.
Repair means redefining roles consciously, restoring cooperation deliberately, and deciding that dysfunction stops being inherited.

Why This Chapter Matters

Wealth cannot stabilize where trust is broken.
Leadership cannot grow where authority is confused.
Unity cannot form where exhaustion dominates.
The family is not the only institution.
But it is the first multiplier.
If the foundation is repaired, everything built above it stands stronger.
If it is avoided, nothing lasts.

Where This Leaves Us

We now understand the structural damage to the family.
From here, the work changes.
From diagnosis to reconstruction.
From naming to building.
From survival to strategy.

Chapter 6: Division by Design

Once a foundation is repaired, the real threat emerges: alignment. The next chapter reveals why unity has always been interrupted before it could mature. Division was engineered, incentivized, and internalized, not to destroy people outright, but to prevent them from moving together.

Chapter 6 – Division by Design
Unity by Choice

Division has never been an accident in our history.
It has always been a strategy.
When pressure increases, unity does not naturally rise. It is disrupted, fragmented, and redirected with precision. Not loudly. Quietly. Efficiently.
This chapter exists to name how that disruption works, why it feels personal, and why it has lasted so long.
Because when people fight each other, power remains untouched.
And when people align, power is forced to respond.

Unity Is the Real Threat

Unity has never been dangerous because it is emotional.
It is dangerous because it is operational.
When people align across differences, coordinate resources, and move with shared intent, dependency weakens. Circulation replaces extraction. Influence consolidates instead of dissipating. Fragmentation is unsustainable. Collapse follows.
That is why unity is rarely attacked directly.
It is fractured quietly.
Power does not suppress unity head-on. It rewards division instead.
Separation is incentivized by identity, class, role, and ideology, then framed as natural, personal, or inevitable. As long as people remain divided, pressure can be applied without resistance.
Unity without structure is tolerated.
Unity with coordination is resisted.
This deals with lived experience, not theory.
It is mechanical.
Unity does not require agreement on everything. It requires movement together where survival and power are at stake.

How Division Was Built

Division did not begin with conflict.
It began with categories.
Artificial distinctions turned hierarchy into something that felt normal and competition into something that felt necessary. Instead of building shared capacity, people were trained to compete for proximity. Access was made scarce by design. Approval became currency.
Over time, division stopped feeling imposed.
It began to feel personal.
That is how structure becomes psychology.

Proximity to Power: The Original Template

This was never about location.
It was about proximity.
Conditional safety was offered in exchange for obedience. Punishment was absorbed in exchange for survival. Both groups were controlled. Only one was placed close enough to be visible.
Visibility created resentment, not because proximity created power, but because the system itself remained distant and untouchable. Anger needs a target. Established frameworks redirect the cost to whoever is closest.
If you have ever felt more frustration toward someone one step ahead than toward a system ten steps above, this is where that pattern was trained.
Proximity was mistaken for power.
Resentment was redirected sideways.
Division became self-sustaining.

The Same Structure, New Uniforms

The structure never disappeared.
It changed clothes.
Today, it shows up as corporate versus street, professional versus blue collar, respectable versus problematic. One side is granted conditional approval. The other absorbs scrutiny and blame.
Professionalism is mistaken for superiority instead of adaptation.
Survival is judged as failure instead of resilience.
Respectability becomes a gate instead of a shield.
As long as resentment stays horizontal, hierarchy remains intact.

Color as Access, Not Beauty

This was never about beauty.
It was always about access.
Lighter skin was treated as a shortcut to trust, opportunity, and legitimacy. Darker skin was treated as distance, suspicion, and threat. Not because of character, but because proximity to whiteness was equated with proximity to safety.
That hierarchy did not vanish.
It was absorbed.
It still shapes who is believed, who is doubted, who is forgiven, and who is punished first. It shows up when:
- Lighter skin is read as professional rather than conditioned
- Darker skin is read as dangerous rather than experienced
- Bias is dismissed as preference instead of recognized as a pattern
- Proximity to approval is mistaken for protection

The focus here is understanding, not assigning fault.

It is about recognition.
Colorism survives when it is treated as personal taste instead of inherited hierarchy. Until that structure is named, damage continues sideways while the system remains untouched.

Educated Versus Uncredentialed

This was never about intelligence.
It was about recognition.
Formal education became the gatekeeper to legitimacy while access to credentials remained uneven by design. Those excluded were framed as inferior rather than blocked.
Intelligence was filtered, not measured.
Skill without certification was treated as luck.
Wisdom without paperwork was dismissed.
Lived experience was reduced to an anecdote.
Both forms of intelligence are real.
Only one is routinely respected.
This division teaches people to defend knowledge instead of circulating it. To talk past one another instead of building together. As long as legitimacy is granted by institutions instead of outcomes, collective capacity remains fragmented.

Respectable Versus Radical

This was never about behavior.
It was about the threat level.
Those who complied were rewarded with conditional acceptance.
Anyone who challenged the arrangements of power was labeled dangerous.
Respectability became currency.
Silence became safety.
The system does not fear noise.
It fears coordination.
That is why individual success is celebrated while collective action is questioned. Why outspoken individuals are tolerated until they organize others. Why movements are praised symbolically but resisted structurally.
Respectability fragments resistance.
Coordination forces a response.

Men Versus Women

This was never about gender.
It was about fragmentation.

Strength was separated from nurture. Leadership from care. Provision from presence. Men were trained to carry weight without softness. Women were trained to carry everything else without support.

Pain that should have been processed together was redirected sideways.

If you have ever felt unsupported while standing next to someone who felt the same, this is why.

The system did not need men and women to hate each other.

It only needed them misaligned.

Fragmentation weakens families.

Partnership builds legacy.

How Division Is Maintained

Division is reinforced through incentives.

Access to housing, employment, safety, and legitimacy is often conditioned on separation. Cooperation threatens those incentives. Competition protects them.

This reflects pattern, not speculation.

It is incentive design.

Division feels emotional because trauma trains people to prioritize safety over strategy. Under pressure, disagreement feels dangerous. Difference feels personal.

While people debate identity, structures make decisions.

False Unity Versus Functional Unity

False unity demands silence.

Functional unity requires alignment.

Alignment is built through shared goals, clear roles, accountability, and the ability to disagree without fragmentation.

Unity without structure collapses.

Structure without trust never forms.

Unity must be chosen.

Disciplined.

Maintained.

What Power Actually Fears

Power does not fear anger.

It has learned to monetize it.

Power does not fear awareness.

It has learned to absorb it.

Power fears organized clarity.

People who understand the system, trust each other, coordinate action, and build institutions.

Division keeps people busy.
Alignment changes conditions.

Where This Leaves Us

We now understand how division was engineered, how pain was redirected, and how unity was interrupted.
But unity without capacity collapses.
And capacity without discipline fades.
Before we build, strength must be restored.

Chapter 7: The Education Trap

After division comes sorting.
Chapter 7 examines one of the most effective tools ever used to assign value, legitimacy, and direction: education. Not learning, but filtering. Not wisdom, but approval. This chapter exposes how intelligence was ranked to control access and limit scale.

PART 2 — The Design: How They Engineered Our Limits

Chapter 7 – The Education Trap
How Schooling Trains Compliance, Not Power

The mistake has never been participation.
The mistake has been submission.
School was never meant to be a savior.
It was meant to be a tool.
Somewhere along the way, we were taught to confuse access with leverage. To believe that if we followed the path, earned the grades, and collected the credentials, power would eventually follow. But grades began questioning our intelligence instead of sharpening our strategy. Credentials became identity instead of utility.
The education system does not need to be destroyed to be defeated.
It needs to be outgrown.
Chess is not about flipping the board.
It is about positioning.
School provides access.
It does not provide dominance.
The real question is not whether we should use the system.
The real question is how we use it without letting it define us.

Education Was Never Neutral

Education has always done more than teach information. It has sorted people, filtered legitimacy, and decided who would be heard before they ever spoke.
Learning and recognition were separated on purpose.
Intelligence has always existed in our communities. What was restricted was institutional permission. Degrees did not replace hierarchy. They refined it. They decided whose knowledge counted and whose wisdom needed translation before it was respected.
This is why two people can say the same thing, and only one is believed. Education does not just prepare people to participate. It determines who architects outcomes, who administers control, and who is allowed to question the design. That distinction changes everything.

School Measures Performance, Not Potential

This is what must be understood early, clearly, and without confusion.
School measures:
- Behavior in a system
- Compliance with structure
- Ability to perform under rules

School does not measure:
- Intelligence

- Vision
- Leadership capacity
- Long-term impact

Grades describe how well you function inside a framework.
They do not define how far you can build beyond it.
Authority inside the school is contextual.
It is not absolute.
Learning is permanent.
School is temporary.
A child who understands this does not collapse under labels. An adult who understands this does not confuse credentials with worth.

The Parallel Education Model

Every community that has ever accumulated lasting power understood one thing clearly: no single institution is sufficient. Education has always operated along parallel tracks of access and control. Formal schooling provides access, credentials, and baseline skills. Family and community are responsible for everything else. When a household outsources identity, discipline, leadership, and internal order to institutions that were never designed to provide them, the outcome is predictable. School must become the floor, not the ceiling. When that shift happens, the trap loses its grip.
School handles:
- Literacy
- Numeracy
- Credentials
- Access

Family and community must handle:
- Identity
- Systems literacy
- Economic intelligence
- Leadership development
- Discipline and emotional regulation

When school becomes the floor instead of the ceiling, the trap loses its grip.
The shift is strategic, not oppositional.
Dominance does not come from rejection.
It comes from parallel development.

Reframing Intelligence

Intelligence does not live on a test. It reveals itself in how people solve problems, recognize patterns, lead others, create under constraint, navigate complex social environments, and adapt when conditions change. A system built to reward silence, compliance, and memorization will consistently misread brilliance as disruption. That does not mean intelligence is missing.

It means it is being measured incorrectly. Our responsibility is not to force children to contort themselves to fit a narrow definition of intelligence, but to help them extract value from the system without surrendering their identity. When brilliance is treated as a problem instead of a resource, it does not disappear. It relocates, often into frustration, disengagement, or self-doubt.

How We Use School Without Being Used by It

School should be treated as a tool, not an authority over identity or destiny. It functions as a credential pipeline, a place to acquire foundational skills, and a temporary phase of development. It is not a moral judge, a measure of worth, or a life sentence. Grades do not define intelligence. Educational pathways should never be chosen without understanding how they connect to real leverage. Debt should never be accepted without a clear plan for how it will be used and repaid. When education is positioned correctly, it becomes useful. When it is misunderstood, it becomes a quiet form of submission.

Same Country, Different Training

The design is uneven by intent.
A fifth grader in one zip code is trained to think, question, and lead.
A fifth grader in another is trained to comply, repeat, and stay quiet.
Same country.
Same grade.
Completely different outcomes.
That is not a coincidence; it's by design.

Tiger Woods and the Myth of Neutrality

Exceptional outcomes almost always begin before institutions get involved. Tiger Woods did not emerge from conditions organized around Black excellence. He emerged from a family structure that assumed full responsibility for his development.
Golf was not built for him.
The culture was not neutral.
The pipeline was not welcoming.
His parents understood that.
Golf is the lens, not the lesson.
It is about structure.
Tiger's father did not hope the system would figure his son out. He assessed the environment and built something parallel. His mother was part of that structure. This was the result of alignment.
Discipline.

Focus.
Emotional regulation.
Pressure tolerance.
Without that foundation, Tiger would have been labeled early, redirected quietly, and filtered into a lane that matched expectations instead of capacity.
That is how brilliance disappears without theft ever being named.
School provided access.
Home provided an advantage.
One without the other would have failed.

The Skills That Actually Create Power

Every household must supplement schooling with education in:
- Money flow and ownership
- Contracts and negotiation
- Business structures
- Technology leverage
- Legal awareness
- Media literacy

These are not advanced topics.
They are survival skills in the current landscape.
Without them, education produces dependency rather than dominance.

From Compliance to Capacity

School trains compliance because compliance keeps institutions running. That is not accidental, and it is not personal. Compliance produces reliable workers, predictable outcomes, and minimal disruption. Capacity produces something else entirely. Capacity allows people to think long-term, delay gratification, coordinate with others, build institutions, and transfer knowledge across generations. Compliance can keep you employed, and there is nothing wrong with that. But capacity allows people to shape conditions instead of merely surviving inside them. Power does not fear obedience. They fear people who understand the mechanics of control and can operate beyond them.

What Dominance Actually Looks Like

Dominance is not aggression, volume, or visibility. It is optionality. It shows up as multiple income paths instead of dependence on one. Ownership instead of access. Skills that transfer across industries. Families that teach what schools omit. Communities that coordinate instead of compete. Real dominance is quiet. It does not need applause. It does not wait for permission. It does not announce itself until conditions have already shifted.

Why This Chapter Matters

People who misunderstand education chase approval forever.
People who understand design eventually determine outcomes.
Education was never the enemy.
Ignorance of how education functions was.
We do not abandon school.
We transcend its limits.

Where This Leaves Us

Once the trap is exposed, creativity reappears.

Chapter 8: Innovation Is Our Inheritance

What was suppressed was never capacity.
It was permission.
Innovation was not missing.
It was constrained.
The next chapter shows what happens when creativity is no longer filtered through approval and is finally structured for ownership.

Chapter 8 – Innovation Is Our Inheritance
Why Creativity Was Never the Problem

One of the most persistent lies we inherited is this: that applied intelligence belongs to someone else. That originality is rare. That invention is elite. That leadership is reserved.

None of that is true.

Our capacity to solve, design, and build did not skip us. What most of us learned early was not a lack of ability, but a habit of lowering our ideas before anyone else could reject them. What was taken was never intelligence. It was ownership.

Creation Predates Permission

Long before patents, venture capital, or formal pipelines, we built solutions under constraint. We produced outcomes without infrastructure, architecture without backing, tools without factories, and processes without capital. Problem-solving thrives under pressure, not because pressure is good, but because necessity demands intelligence.

What history often labels as resilience was large-scale problem-solving without recognition.

Ingenuity Survived What Freedom Did Not

Even when ownership was illegal, constructive ability did not disappear. People engineered food networks from scraps, communication through rhythm and coded language, medicine through plant knowledge, and logistics through informal economies. This was not folklore. It was applied intelligence without credit.

Applied intelligence without ownership always benefits whoever controls the outcome.

Why Creation Was Allowed but Ownership Was Not

The critical distinction is this. Ingenuity is often permitted. Control is restricted. Output can be used. Ownership cannot.

Creation was tolerated if credit could be reassigned, profit extracted, and narratives rewritten. That is why invention is often separated from the inventor in historical records. The work was allowed. The authority was not.

How Building Was Reframed

Another subtle shift followed. The ability to build was reframed as talent rather than discipline, genius rather than process, and luck rather than structure. Building began to feel exceptional instead of trainable.
When capacity is mystified, most people opt out before they begin. That moment is physical. Hesitation. Tightening. The decision to stay quiet rather than risk visibility. Labor-first frameworks benefit when people police themselves.
Think about how many ideas you have had that never left your head because failing felt more dangerous than staying silent.

The Cost of Interrupting Inheritance

The capacity to build is not only individual. It is cultural. When transmission breaks, skills are not passed down. Experiments are not scaled. Failure is not normalized. Progress resets every generation.
Each generation starts over, not because ability is absent, but because continuity was interrupted.
That interruption is why families restart businesses instead of expanding them, why skills die with one person, and why momentum keeps collapsing just as it begins to compound.

Why Building Feels Risky Today

When failure has historically been punished harder, experimentation shrinks. When mistakes carry higher costs, applied intelligence gets redirected. Energy flows toward visibility, hustle, and expression, while infrastructure, structure, and ownership are neglected.
Not because intelligence disappeared, but because structure never arrived. The nervous system remembers consequences even when context changes.

Where Applied Intelligence Learned to Hide

Most people did not stop building. They stopped sharing.
Ideas stayed in notebooks. Plans stayed unfinished. Conversations ended with "never mind." Not because the ideas were weak, but because experience taught that visibility had a cost.

Creation Without Infrastructure Is Exhausting

Ideas without support burn people out. Lone builders carry everything themselves and eventually collapse under the weight. Burnout, endless restarting, hustling without scale, and carrying ideas without protection all come from the same problem.
Sustainable building requires capital, collaboration, protection, and patience. Without infrastructure, builders become lone heroes instead of architects.
Heroism does not scale. Infrastructure does.

What This Chapter Is Reclaiming

This chapter is not arguing that we can build. It is asserting that we always have. The question was never originality. The question was control.
Control requires ownership, coordination, and long-term thinking. Those are learned. Those are buildable.

Why This Matters Before Power and Wealth

The capacity to build fuel business formation, economic leverage, political influence, and narrative control. But ability without direction disperses energy.
Before we talk about voting blocs, money, or institutions, building capacity must be anchored as an inheritance, not an exception.

Where This Leaves Us

The myth of deficiency is dismantled. The problem was never intelligence. Never creativity. Never work ethic. The problem was the interruption.
Pause here.
Where has your ability to build been expressed but never supported long enough to become ownership? Not because you lacked capacity, but because the structure was never built.

The Power Vote

Innovation without leverage remains vulnerable. Chapter 9 moves from creativity to influence. It examines how power is translated into policy, protection, and permanence.
Voting here is not symbolic.
It is strategic.
This chapter is about understanding how decisions are actually enforced.

Chapter 9 – The Power Vote
Why Voting Without Structure Fails

"Power concedes nothing without a demand. It never did, and it never will."
— Frederick Douglass

Frederick Douglass was not offering inspiration.
He was explaining mechanics.
Power does not move because it is persuaded.
It moves because pressure makes immobility costly.
Voting, when understood correctly, is not a moral performance.
It is leverage.
And leverage only works when it is organized, coordinated, and disciplined.

Why the Vote Was Feared

The vote was never feared because of feelings.
It was feared because of the numbers with direction.
When voting is unified, predictable, and strategic, it forces negotiation.
When voting is fragmented, emotional, symbolic, or sporadic, it gets ignored.
Douglass spoke about demands, not loyalty, because he understood a rule most people are never taught.
Power does not respond to passion.
It responds to pressure.

Participation Is Not Power

High turnout alone does not equal influence.
Without coordination, participation becomes noise. Loud for a moment, forgotten by the next news cycle.
Power does not measure output.
It measures structure.
That is why power asks different questions.
Can this group move together?
Unity creates force.
Individuals cancel each other out.
Coordination multiplies impact.
Power cannot negotiate with confusion.
It responds to discipline.
A group that moves together signals cost.
And cost forces response.

Can This Group Withhold Support?

Leverage only exists where refusal is possible.
Support that cannot be withdrawn is not leverage.
It is permission.
If support is guaranteed, negotiation disappears.
The ability to say no introduces risk.
Risk forces attention.

Can This Group Sustain Pressure Over Time?

Power is patient.
Most movements fail not because they are wrong, but because they are temporary.
Outrage fades.
Headlines move on.
Power waits.
Endurance, not emotion, forces change.

Can This Group Remember and Punish Betrayal?

Memory creates accountability.
Power depends on short attention spans.
When promises are forgotten, the system resets in favor of those already in control.
When memory is enforced, power becomes constrained.
If the answer to these questions is no, attention fades.
Not because the issue does not matter.
But because the pressure does not last.
Power does not abandon worthy causes.
It abandons unreliable ones.

Why Coordination Is So Hard for Us

Coordination requires trust.
Trust requires safety.
And safety has never been guaranteed.
For Black communities, moving together has historically carried risk.
Leaders were targeted.
Groups were infiltrated.
Movements were punished.
Promises were broken.
Fragmentation did not come from apathy.
It came from protection.
When unity feels dangerous, individuality feels safer.

When betrayal has history, loyalty becomes cautious.
When disappointment repeats, memory becomes fatigue.
Power exploits this.
Not by inventing division, but by leaning into wounds that already exist.
The outcome is shaped by structure, not morality.
It is conditioning.
But conditioning explains behavior.
It does not change outcomes.

Why Individual Voting Narratives Fail

Modern political messaging flatters the individual.
"Vote your conscience."
"Use your voice."
"Make your choice."
These messages feel empowering.
They are strategically weak.
Power is collective.
One vote expresses values.
Millions of coordinated votes create demands.
A single person can protest.
A disciplined bloc can negotiate.

The Illusion of Representation

Representation is often mistaken for control.
Seeing someone who looks like you in office does not guarantee:
- Policy leverage
- Budget authority
- Agenda control
- Enforcement power

Representation without accountability becomes symbolism.
Symbols inspire.
They do not govern.
Power responds to organized interests, not shared identity.

Why Predictable Votes Lose Leverage

Predictability weakens negotiation.
When support is assumed, concessions disappear.
Power does not reward loyalty.
It exploits certainty.
The groups with the most influence are not the most faithful.
They are the most organized and conditional.
A demand without consequence is not a demand. It is a wish.

How Voting Power Was Neutralized

Predictability did not happen by accident.
District lines were redrawn.
Access was restricted.
Election rules shifted quietly.
Local influence was diluted upward.
Participation remained visible.
Leverage disappeared.
That is not apathy.
That is neutralization.
And neutralization works best when people stop organizing and start reacting.

How Power Decides Whether to Respond

Power watches behavior.
Who remembers promises.
Who forgets them.
Who sustains pressure.
Who burns out.
Promises remembered create expectation.
Promises forgotten dissolve into speeches.
Budgets reveal priorities.
Delays reveal avoidance.
Early actions expose sincerity.
Private disappointment is easy to ignore.
Public accountability creates records.
Outrage passes.
Pressure endures.
No consequences mean no concessions.
That rule never changes.

How Issues Rise or Disappear

Issues do not rise because they are urgent.
They rise because ignoring them becomes costly.
Cost is created through organization.
Unified voices matter more than scattered complaints.
Local pressure matters more than distant outrage.
Sustained presence matters more than viral moments.
Ten disciplined people who return, remember, and repeat will move policy faster than a thousand who appear once and vanish.
Power responds to reliability.

Local Power Is the Missing Link

National politics dominate attention.
Local politics shape conditions.
School boards determine knowledge.
Zoning determines opportunity.
Judges and prosecutors determine enforcement.
City councils determine budgets, contracts, housing, and priorities.
Ignoring local power while chasing national symbolism leaves communities reactive instead of positioned.
Power that begins locally scales upward.
Power that skips local ground remains symbolic.

Voting Is Not the Toolbox

Voting is not power by itself.
It is the trigger.
Power is built through:
- Organized blocs
- Institutional presence
- Economic leverage
- Public accountability
- Disciplined coordination
- Sustained memory

Voting activates leverage only when connected to structure.
Voting is not the weapon.
Structure is.

Why This Chapter Comes Before Money and Health

Political leverage determines:
- Where resources flow
- Which laws are enforced
- Who is protected
- Who is left exposed

Without political literacy, gains in wealth and health remain fragile.
Strategy protects progress.

Pause

Before moving on, ask yourself:
- Where do I participate without coordinating?
- Where have I mistaken visibility for leverage?
- Awareness comes before strategy.

Where This Leaves Us

We now understand:
- How participation is neutralized
- How predictability weakens leverage
- How accountability is enforced
- How power evaluates seriousness

The final system completes the loop.

A population that is exhausted, unhealthy, distracted, and medicated cannot sustain pressure, memory, or coordination.

Power counts on fatigue.

Health Is Liberation

No movement survives without bodies that can sustain it.

Chapter 10 connects physical health to freedom. Exhaustion is not accidental. Illness is not neutral.

This chapter reframes wellness as infrastructure, not lifestyle, and shows how liberation fails when the body is neglected.

Chapter 10 – Health Is Liberation
Why the Body Became a Battlefield

Health is the quiet foundation beneath every form of power.
Before money.
Before politics.
Before institutions.
Before strategy.
The body comes first.
In America, health is usually framed as personal responsibility: eat better, exercise more, manage stress. That framing is incomplete and dangerous. Health is not just individual behavior. It is the result of environment, pressure, access, education, and exposure layered over time. When the same communities experience the same illnesses generation after generation, coincidence is no longer a serious explanation.
This chapter is not about shame. It is about survival, stamina, joy, and legacy. Because freedom requires energy. And energy lives in the body.

Illness Is Not Random

Patterns tell the truth.
Black Americans experience higher rates of hypertension, diabetes, heart disease, stroke, kidney failure, autoimmune conditions, maternal mortality, shortened life expectancy, and cognitive decline. These patterns do not exist because of weakness. They exist because of repeated exposure to stress, poor nutrition environments, disrupted sleep, environmental hazards, and unequal access to preventative care.
You do not get mass illness without mass exposure. And exposure is rarely accidental.
The body responds to what it is consistently asked to endure.
Heart disease deserves to be named directly. For Black men, it remains one of the leading causes of death, not because of weak hearts, but because of accumulated strain. Elevated blood pressure, unmanaged inflammation, poor sleep, chronic stress, limited preventative care, and delayed treatment converge over time.
Symptoms are ignored, minimized, or normalized until damage is already advanced.
Chest tightness is brushed off as indigestion.
Fatigue is mistaken for hustle.
Shortness of breath is blamed on age or weight.
Annual checkups are postponed.
Warning signs are endured quietly.
What gets labeled as masculinity is often exposure.
And when care finally comes, it often arrives late.

Stress Is a Biological Tax

Stress is not just emotional strain. It is a physiological condition.
When the body stays in survival mode, cortisol remains elevated, inflammation increases, immune function weakens, blood pressure rises, and decision-making narrows.
These effects are consequences of chronic stress, not mental weakness.
It is biology working exactly as designed under threat.
A nervous system under constant pressure prioritizes survival over strategy. Short-term relief becomes more attractive than long-term repair. Over time, people stop expecting full health and settle for "manageable."
That behavior signals an adaptive response to exhaustion.
But adaptation carries a cost.

Food Is Infrastructure

Food is often discussed as a preference. In reality, it is infrastructure.
When entire communities are saturated with highly processed foods, excess sugar, refined carbohydrates, seed oils, preservatives, and sodium-heavy meals, choice becomes constrained long before a decision is ever made.
Cheap food is not cheap.
Its cost is deferred.
The issue is structural, not cultural. Preparation methods, consumption patterns, and engineered substitutions are the real drivers.
This design does not require conspiracy.
It only requires incentives.
Illness creates demand.
Demand sustains industries.

Metabolic Breakdown Is the Common Thread

Many chronic conditions share overlapping roots: insulin resistance, chronic inflammation, disrupted sleep, prolonged stress, and poor recovery. This does not mean every illness has one cause. It means the body breaks down along predictable lines when pressure is constant.
Some researchers believe insulin resistance in the brain may contribute to cognitive decline and Alzheimer's disease, which is why you may hear it referred to as "Type 3 Diabetes." Not because it is the same disease, but because energy regulation in the brain appears impaired over time.
This breakdown does not happen suddenly. It develops quietly.
Over years.

Healthcare Is Not the Same as Health

The healthcare system excels at intervention, but it struggles with prevention.
Treatment generates revenue; prevention reduces it. As a result, symptoms are often managed while root causes remain untouched. Medication can be lifesaving, but the danger begins when it becomes the first response instead of the informed response. Relief replaces understanding. People stay functional, but never fully well.
This reflects incentive structures, not individual doctors.

Medical Mistrust Has a History

Mistrust did not appear out of nowhere. It was taught through experimentation without consent, dismissal of pain, unequal treatment, and unequal outcomes. Skepticism became rational. But mistrust carries a cost. Delayed care worsens outcomes. Avoidance compounds damage.
The environment created mistrust and then blamed people for responding to it. Understanding this history is necessary, but it cannot be where the story ends.

Hydration Is a Daily Exposure

Water is not magic. It is exposure. The body regulates acidity well; what wears it down is constant correction. Sugary drinks, energy drinks, artificial sweeteners, and stimulant-heavy liquids keep the body working overtime just to maintain balance. Over time, that adds strain.
Clean, mineral-containing water places less demand on the body, not because it cures disease, but because it does not add unnecessary burden.
Hydration is not about chasing perfect pH. It is about reducing workload.

Health Determines Capacity

Health shapes energy, focus, emotional regulation, endurance, and longevity. A tired body struggles to organize. An inflamed nervous system struggles to lead. The issue is capacity math. When bodies never fully recover, attention shortens, curiosity fades, and complexity feels overwhelming. In that state, authority becomes easier to trust than investigation.
This is how power quietly stays put.

Healthcare as the Choke Point

Healthcare is not a benefit. It is a bargaining chip. In the United States, access to affordable health insurance is tied primarily to full-time employment, leaving part-time, gig, and contract workers exposed by design. Coverage is sold as protection, yet constantly challenged in practice. Premiums are collected on time; care is debated later. People do not just pay for insurance. They fight it. They argue over what is covered, appeal what is denied, and wait while bills accumulate. The customer pays monthly, but still has to prove they deserve care when their body fails. This turns health into leverage. People stay in jobs they have outgrown not because the work sustains them, but because losing coverage feels dangerous. One diagnosis can erase years of saving.
One gap in coverage can become lifelong debt. So people stay. They comply. They delay care. They ration health. This keeps people productive but anxious, employed but controlled. Survival mode deepens.

Accountability Is Not Blame

We eat poorly. We skip preventive care. We normalize habits that shorten our lives. These patterns formed under pressure. They made sense at the time. But bodies do not negotiate with nostalgia. What began as survival has become a cost.
You cannot organize while exhausted. You cannot lead while inflamed. You cannot build a strategy while sedated.
Cruelty has nothing to do with it. Biology does.

Agency Returns Through Awareness

Annual checkups are not paranoia. Knowing your numbers is not betrayal. Asking questions is not disrespect. If you do not understand what is happening in your body, someone else will manage it for you, often with medication, rarely with explanation.
Medication has its place. Understanding must come first.

Where Support Actually Exists

Information alone does not change lives. Access does.
For many of us, the challenge has never been caring about our health. It has been knowing where to turn, who to trust, and how to move through conditions that were never built with us in mind.
Support does exist. Some of it is rooted in our communities, led by people who understand our history, our bodies, and our realities.
To avoid overwhelming this chapter with lists and links, all health and wellness resources referenced here live in one place.

Scan the QR code below to explore Black-led health education, mental and emotional wellness support, guidance on navigating care and coverage, and community-based tools designed to support informed decision-making. These resources are not prescriptions. They are starting points designed to support informed questions, better access, and healthier outcomes over time.

Use what supports you. Leave what doesn't.

Why Health Comes Before Money

Without health:
- Progress collapses
- Strategy weakens
- Endurance disappears

We could not talk about wealth before restoring capacity.
Health is the foundation beneath the foundation.

Pause

Before moving on, ask yourself:
- Where have I normalized feeling unwell?
- What habits am I calling "just life"?
- What would change if my body had more capacity?

Awareness comes before action.

Money 101: Financial Literacy as Liberation

Health without resources is fragile.
Chapter 11 introduces financial literacy not as aspiration, but as defense. Money is not morality. It is mechanism. This chapter breaks the silence around economics and exposes how ignorance was made expensive on purpose.

Chapter 11 – Financial Literacy
Why Working Hard Was Never the Plan

Money is emotional for most people.
Not because money is confusing, but because money was never explained honestly.
What we were taught sounded like wisdom:
Work hard.
Save what you can.
Do not talk about money.
Be grateful for the opportunity.
What we were not taught was how money actually behaves.
This chapter exists to separate financial truth from financial folklore.
For generations, many of us were told that discipline alone would close the gap. If we worked harder, budgeted better, and stayed patient, stability would eventually arrive. When it did not, the blame quietly shifted to character instead of structure, effort instead of design.
This chapter challenges that framing.
Seeds in the Soil is not a motivational book, and this is not a motivational chapter. It is not written for speed, entertainment, or easy agreement. It is a structural examination of how money actually moves, how systems extract value, and why effort without ownership often leads to exhaustion instead of freedom.
This chapter assumes you are capable of responsibility.
It does not ask you to be perfect.
It asks you to be informed.

Why Income Never Built Wealth

Income is labor converted into cash. Wealth is ownership converted into leverage. They are not the same. Income stops when labor stops, while wealth compounds even in your absence. For generations, we were taught to chase income while being denied ownership, and that was not accidental. A system can survive high incomes. It cannot survive widespread ownership.

What This Looks Like in Real Life

Here is what chasing income without ownership looks like in real life. You get a raise and feel relief, briefly. The check is bigger, but rent adjusts. Insurance increases. Groceries climb. Subscriptions creep in. The lifestyle stretches to meet the income, and the margin disappears again.
Nothing went wrong. The design worked.
Income makes life manageable. Ownership makes life negotiable. Without ownership, every increase in income simply feeds structures you do not control.

Cash Flow vs Control

Cash flow helps you breathe.
Control determines your future.
Many people earn well and still feel trapped because they do not own the structures they pay into, do not control the rules of exchange, and do not benefit from appreciation.
Money without control feels unstable.
That instability breeds anxiety, not freedom.

Why Saving Alone Was Never Enough

Saving is defensive.
It protects against emergencies.
It does not create leverage.
In an economy built on inflation and asset growth, saved cash quietly loses power over time.
Saving is necessary.
It is not sufficient.
Without ownership, saving becomes waiting.

The Bank App Moment

Most people don't realize they're trapped until a quiet moment reveals it.
You open your banking app. The numbers look okay, not great, not terrible. You mentally sort bills. Decide which one can wait. You tell yourself you'll "catch up next month."
That moment is not a failure. Its dependence revealing itself.
When your entire life is synchronized to a deposit schedule, freedom is conditional. Miss one check, and the illusion dissolves.

Inflation, Taxes, and the Quiet Squeeze

Inflation is not just prices going up. It is pressure closing in. Each year, a little more of the check disappears before life even begins. Groceries cost more. Rent climbs. Insurance rises. Gas fluctuates but never really comes back down. Fees appear where none existed before. What used to fit no longer does. Wages rarely move the same way, and when they do, it feels like progress for a moment until the math catches up. Raises arrive late and leave early. Inflation collects first. Taxes do not pause. Bills do not negotiate. Savings lose strength sitting still. So even when income increases, life feels tighter, not because you mismanaged, but because the structure is calibrated that way. You are running harder just to stay in the same place. Financial struggle is often misread as illiteracy, when it is engineered friction. Inflation punishes cash. Taxes drain labor. Ownership shields value. This is not an opinion. It is how the system sustains itself.

Why It Feels Like You're Losing Ground

This is why so many people say, "I make more than I ever have, but I feel poorer."
You're not imagining it.
When labor is taxed first, cash is devalued second, and ownership is delayed or denied, output increases while leverage shrinks. You are running faster inside a narrowing lane.
The problem is not spending habits. The problem is position.

Money Is a Language

Money is a language, and it follows rules. Not moral rules, but mechanical ones. Assets grow or decay. Liabilities drain or amplify. Cash flows stagnate. Appreciation compounds. Depreciation erodes. When you do not understand the rules, you rely on translators, and translators charge fees. That is how confusion becomes expensive. Financial literacy does not make people wealthy. It makes them harder to exploit. Once people understand how money behaves, shame dissolves. Decisions slow down. Questions sharpen. Literacy restores choice.

Why Confusion Is Expensive

Confusion is not neutral.
Every time you don't understand a fee, an interest rate, a term, or a contract, someone else profits from your uncertainty.
Financial structures do not require ignorance; they monetize it. Literacy interrupts extraction.

Reader Tools: Where Practical Support Actually Exists

Understanding money is one step. Accessing clear, trustworthy tools is another.
To avoid overwhelming this chapter with lists and links, all financial education resources connected to this book live in one place.
Scan the QR code below to explore tools designed to support financial literacy, system awareness, ownership pathways, and informed decision-making.
These resources are not promises. They are frameworks.
Use them to ask better questions. Slow down decisions. Recognize traps before they close.

Literacy doesn't make you wealthy. It makes you harder to exploit.

What the Tools Are Meant to Do

The resource you just accessed is not meant to make you rich. It is meant to make you literate. Literacy means understanding how money moves, recognizing extraction before it happens, asking better questions, and seeing traps early instead of explaining them later. The focus here is clarity, not motivation. Clarity removes shame, restores choice, and shifts power back to the person holding the information.

Money Is Not Moral, It Is Mechanical

We were taught to see money as a reflection of character, and that framing keeps people stuck. Money is not good or evil. It follows rules. When those rules are unknown, the system collects penalties. When they are understood, leverage becomes possible. Moralizing money creates shame.
Understanding money creates options.

Why Blame Was Always Misplaced

For too long, financial struggle was explained as:
- Laziness

- Poor choices
- Lack of discipline

That explanation ignores access, information, and structure.
When rules are hidden, failure is predictable.
Exposure creates responsibility.
But it also creates freedom.

This Is Where Agency Actually Begins

Agency is not confidence. It is competence. Once people understand the difference between income and wealth, assets and liabilities, credit and cash, ownership and consumption, they stop negotiating against themselves. That shift is quiet, but permanent. This is why this chapter appears here and nowhere else. Money could not be taught before identity was stabilized, pain was named, and health capacity was restored, because money magnifies whatever already exists. Without literacy, money amplifies chaos. With literacy, money amplifies intention.

Where This Leaves Us

We now understand:
- How identity was distorted
- How systems extracted value
- How health impacts capacity
- How money mechanics work

The next step is ownership.
Not hustle.
Not fantasy.
Structure.

Business Ownership

Literacy without ownership stalls.
Chapter 12 moves from understanding money to controlling flow.
Employment creates income. Ownership creates leverage. This chapter reframes business as a survival strategy, not a status symbol.

Chapter 12 – Business Ownership
From Laborers to Legacy Builders

Business ownership is often sold as freedom. In reality, it is responsibility multiplied.

This chapter exists to tell the truth about ownership, not the fantasy, not the hype, but the structure. For generations, Black labor was dependable while Black ownership was discouraged, blocked, or punished. That separation was not accidental.

Why We Were Trained to Work, Not Own

Labor has always been safe for those in power. Ownership was not. Workers produce value. Owners control it. So we were trained to be excellent employees, to chase income, to respect jobs, and to fear risk. Not because work is dishonorable, but because ownership shifts power.

A system can absorb hard work. It struggles with independence.

How Ownership Was Systematically Blocked

Ownership was not restricted through messaging alone. It was limited in access. Capital was withheld or priced aggressively. Licensing and compliance were made complex and costly. Markets were controlled by gatekeepers with no incentive to widen entry. Failure carried harsher penalties and fewer recovery paths.

Work was permitted. Ownership was monitored.

Over time, entrepreneurship became individualized, underfunded, and isolated. Not because of lack of talent, but because scale, protection, and continuity were denied. Labor remained abundant. Ownership stayed rare.

The Hustle Myth

Hustle culture sells urgency without structure. It glorifies long hours, constant motion, and personal sacrifice. But hustle without durable frameworks leads to burnout, fragile income, inconsistency, and businesses that collapse when the owner rests.

Ownership is not speed. It is repeatability.

Real businesses function through processes, delegation, and disciplined frameworks that operate without constant supervision. That is the difference between income and enterprise.

The W-2 Lifecycle Trap

The W-2 was never designed to make people free. It was designed to keep them functional. Its limits are structural. Most people enter the workforce early and remain there for decades, trading hours for pay, approval for stability, and time for deposits. Taxes are removed before money is touched. Bills are scheduled around pay periods. Life organizes itself around the next check.
Miss one, and the fragility reveals itself.
Plans pause. Anxiety spikes. Choices narrow. What felt like security shows its edge. Over time, inflation rises faster than wages. Housing, food, insurance, and healthcare consume more of each check. Higher pay feels like relief, briefly. Then costs absorb it, and survival takes focus. Bandwidth exhaustion explains this far better than irresponsibility ever could.
When people live in survival mode, long-term planning collapses. Retirement becomes abstract, deferred, and optional. Things rarely settle down.

Why Black Businesses Struggle

Most Black-owned businesses do not struggle because of a lack of intelligence or ability. They struggle because of predictable structural gaps: undercapitalization, no separation between personal and business finances, weak legal structures, no standard operating procedures, no governance, and no succession planning.
These are not character flaws. They are education gaps created by exclusion. And gaps can be closed.

Business is a System, not a Personality

Many businesses are built around one person's energy. That works until sickness, stress, family obligations, or burnout appear. A business that collapses without the owner is not a business. It is a job with added risk. Ownership means building something that survives your absence.

Collective Ownership Was Never the Problem

One of the most persistent myths is that Black people cannot work together. History says otherwise. We built churches, mutual aid societies, insurance collectives, and cooperative enterprises.
What failed was not cooperation. It was protection and continuity.
Solo entrepreneurship is fragile. Shared infrastructure is resilient.

Why Scale Matters More Than Passion

Passion starts things. Organization grows them. Scale requires capital, trust, standardized processes, and long-term thinking. Without scale, businesses remain vulnerable. With scale, they become institutions. Institutions outlive individuals.

Ownership Changes Identity

Ownership changes how people plan, hire, negotiate, and think. It shifts timelines from paychecks to decades. It alters how time, money, and responsibility are understood.
That shift is the beginning of legacy.

Retirement, Debt, and Credit

Survival mode destroys foresight. Retirement used to be structurally supported through pensions. That support was withdrawn and rebranded as personal choice. Many people cannot contribute to retirement accounts because survival consumes the margin. Over time, Social Security became a lifeline rather than a supplement.
What remains is survival planning, not retirement.
It is managed survival.
Debt itself is not the enemy. The question is what the debt produces after it is paid. Consumption debt drains future labor. Asset-backed debt creates capacity. Credit functions as quantified trust. When access is restricted or priced aggressively, opportunity shrinks.
These outcomes were structured, not accidental.

Consumption vs Contribution

A consumer economy needs buyers. An ownership economy needs builders. Consumption is predictable and easy to monetize. Ownership is disruptive. Owners ask different questions, negotiate instead of comply, and think in structures rather than transactions.
Consumption ends at satisfaction. Ownership begins responsibility.

This Is Where Liberation Becomes Infrastructure

Ownership stabilizes families, creates employment, circulates capital, protects culture, and anchors communities. These functions operate at the level of systems.
Liberation without ownership is temporary.
Ownership without discipline collapses.
Both are required.

Reader Tools: Business Ownership

The resource connected to this chapter provides orientation, not shortcuts. It helps readers understand business structures, separate labor from ownership, see where structure determines outcomes more than working harder, and avoid traps before they quietly steal years.

Where This Leaves Us

We now understand why labor was rewarded, why ownership was restricted, why individual success was celebrated while collective scale was undermined, and why the underlying structures were concealed while personal exertion was praised.
The next step is skill. Ownership without skill is fragile. Skill without direction is wasted.

Breaking the Barrel

Ownership exposes the final illusion: individual escape.
Chapter 13 challenges the myth that one person's success equals collective progress. This chapter introduces the necessity of coordination, shared infrastructure, and mutual protection.
Escaping avoids pressure. It does not dismantle what creates it.
Unity does.

PART 3 — The Roots: Healing, Unity & Identity

What a privilege it is to be tired from the work you once prayed for.
What a privilege it is to feel overwhelmed by growth you used to dream about.
What a privilege it is to be challenged by a life you created on purpose.
What a privilege it is to outgrow the things you once settled for.
To be tired from having the thing you once dreamed of doing
is a beautiful blessing.

Chapter 13 – Breaking the Barrel
Why Division Serves the System

There's a story often told about crabs in a barrel. When one crab tries to climb out, the others pull it back down. The story is usually told with judgment, like the crabs are petty, jealous, or broken.
That story is lazy.
Crabs were never meant to live in barrels.
The barrel is the problem, not the crabs.
In the same way, systemic oppression created a barrel for Black people. Tight. Enclosed. Controlled. A space where movement feels dangerous, success feels suspicious, and survival feels competitive. The barrel manufactures scarcity turns neighbors into rivals, and trains people to fight sideways instead of up.
This chapter is not about blaming us for how we learned to survive.
It is about naming the container that taught us to survive this way and deciding whether we will keep living inside it.

Oppression Creates Competition

Scarcity changes behavior.
When resources are consistently restricted, trust erodes. Cooperation weakens. Competition replaces coordination. This response is predictable under sustained pressure, not a cultural flaw.
If you have ever hesitated to share good news with family because you feared resentment instead of celebration, you have felt the barrel.
If you have ever watched someone who looks like you undercut you for approval from someone above you, you have seen the barrel working.
If you have ever felt guilty for wanting more than survival, more than just "making it," you have carried the barrel inside you.
In environments shaped by scarcity, people protect position instead of building capacity. They guard small wins instead of organizing for bigger ones. Not because they lack character, but because they were trained to believe there is never enough to go around.
Jealousy is not the disease.
Competition is not the root problem.
Scarcity is the weapon.

Why We Turn on Each Other

Division is not random.
When control cannot fully suppress a people, fragmentation becomes the strategy.
Roles are split. Narratives are divided. Generations are separated. Men and women are pitted against each other.

Classes are isolated.
Fragmentation weakens trust and destroys coordination. It makes collective power impossible while making individual survival feel urgent.
You see it when older generations dismiss younger ones instead of mentoring them. You see it when Black men and Black women are taught to argue in caricatures instead of standing in partnership. You see it when those who "make it out" are praised for escape but never equipped to stay connected.
When we fight each other, the system does not have to intervene.
The barrel does the work for it.

The Cost of Internalized Scarcity

Scarcity does not just limit resources.
It reshapes identity.
When people are conditioned to believe there will never be enough, the mind adapts:
- There is only room for one
- If they rise, you fall
- If you share, you lose

Under that pressure, mentorship gives way to comparison. Support turns into suspicion. Ego replaces governance. People start measuring themselves against the nearest person instead of questioning the structure above them.
We mistake proximity for threat.
Visibility for safety.
Approval for power.
This mindset is not our fault.
But leaving it unchallenged becomes our responsibility.
Internalized scarcity keeps people small even when opportunity grows. Breaking it requires telling the truth about where these instincts came from and deciding they no longer get to run our future.

Breaking the Barrel Requires Awareness

You cannot dismantle what you refuse to name.
The barrel shows up quietly. Success feels isolating. Progress creates distance. Achievement brings guilt. Growth gets hidden to avoid backlash. These are not personality traits. They are learned behaviors passed down in families, churches, schools, and workplaces that adapted to life inside someone else's container.
Awareness is the first crack in the barrel.
The moment you can say, *this isn't just me. This is conditioning*; you regain choice.
Awareness shifts posture.
From isolation to community.

From fear to collaboration.
From defensiveness to strategy.
You cannot break a barrel you still believe is home.

Unity Is Not Agreement

Unity does not mean sameness.
It means alignment.
Real unity is shared direction, mutual protection, and commitment to a collective future. Disagreement is not the threat. Unmanaged distrust is.
Healthy communities disagree and still move together.
History shows this clearly. Black freedom movements have always begun with alignment. They fracture when ego, exhaustion, outside pressure, and unresolved fear override trust.
The work is not avoiding conflict.
The work is building enough trust that disagreement sharpens the mission instead of sabotaging it.

Why Individual Success Was Never Enough

Individual success can inspire.
It cannot stabilize.
One person escaping a hostile system does not dismantle the system. It exposes how fragile solo success really is. Promotions can be revoked. Contracts can disappear. Narratives can be rewritten overnight.
Individual success proves what is possible.
Collective success proves what is sustainable.
Real transformation requires shared ownership, coordinated leadership, and structures designed to outlast personalities.

What Breaking the Barrel Actually Looks Like

Breaking the barrel does not mean everyone becomes the same.
It means remembering we were never meant to fight each other for air.
The fight for position was learned, not natural. It came from environments where access was limited, protection was absent, and survival felt competitive. When opportunity looks scarce, proximity feels like threat.
Breaking the barrel does not mean everyone becomes the same.
It means remembering we were never meant to fight each other for air.
The fight for position was learned, not natural. It came from environments where access was limited, protection was absent, and survival felt competitive.
Breaking the barrel looks like a collaboration replacing competition. Mentorship replacing comparison. Shared infrastructure instead of an isolated hustle. Collective protection instead of individual defense.

It looks like celebrating growth instead of interrogating it.
It looks like asking, *how can I support?* Instead of *Why them?*
Someone else's rise does not shrink your future unless the barrel is still intact.
Ego asks, *do they see me?*
Legacy asks, *Will this still stand when I'm gone?*
What we build together lasts longer than what we win alone.
Breaking the barrel is not symbolic.
It is behavioral.
It is structural.
It is spiritual.

Reader's Note: Ashe. Amen

Ashe: the power to speak and create.
Amen: confirmation that it is already done.
Together:
The power to declare life and the discipline to build it.
Breathe.
Speak it.
AH-shay. AMEN.
Turn the page not just to read, but to plant.

Where This Leaves Us

Unity collapses without trust.
Chapter 14 addresses the hardest work of all: relearning reliability after betrayal. It focuses on rebuilding confidence between people who were trained to compete, doubt, and withdraw.
Trust repairs the bridge.

Chapter 14 – Trust Repairs the Bridge
Why Healing Is Structural, Not Sentimental

Trust in our community does not break only from outside harm. It fractures when the wounds come from inside our own circles. Not strangers. Family. Friends. Leaders. Institutions that looked familiar and sounded safe. Everyone knows these stories. Money mishandled quietly. Reputations damaged behind closed doors. Promises made publicly and abandoned without repair. These moments are not side notes. They are data points.
Trust does not disappear because people are fragile.
It disappears because betrayal teaches caution.
And caution, repeated long enough, becomes structure.

Why Trust Broke in the First Place

Trust does not collapse suddenly. It erodes.
Each broken promise teaches a lesson.
Each unprotected sacrifice trains restraint.
Each ignored harm rewires expectation.
People do not become guarded because they enjoy distance. They become guarded because openness was punished.
What looks like cynicism is learned conditioning.
When leadership fails to protect, people learn to self-protect. When accountability disappears, people stop investing emotionally. When harm is minimized, people stop risking vulnerability.
Trust did not leave.
It withdrew.

Trauma Teaches People to Self-Insure

Chronic failure reshapes how people survive.
They limit exposure.
They keep plans private.
They rely on themselves.
They brace for disappointment.
Not because they want isolation, but because isolation felt safer.
Self-insurance makes sense under pressure, but it comes with a cost. You cannot scale what you refuse to share. You cannot coordinate what you hide. You cannot build power without pooled risk. When trust remains individual, power remains small. That is why understanding how trust broke matters, not to assign blame, but to make repair possible.

Why Trust Cannot Be Demanded

Trust does not respond to requests. "Just trust us" is not leadership; it is a warning sign. Trust returns only when people see predictable behavior, visible accountability, power restrained by rules, and repair following harm. Charisma does not rebuild trust. Intentions do not rebuild trust. History does not rebuild trust. Structure does.

Repair Requires New Rules, Not Old Memories

Nostalgia cannot repair damage. Remembering how things used to be does nothing for people who were harmed when it mattered. Trust returns through clarity: clear roles, defined authority, transparent decision-making, and consequences that actually occur.
People trust what they can understand. Ambiguity benefits power, not people. Clarity creates stability, and stability restores confidence.

Why Transparency Is Non-Negotiable

Opacity is where abuse hides. Transparency lowers anxiety, disrupts rumors, and prevents resentment from accumulating underground. Healthy systems do not hide the process. They make it visible.
When people understand how decisions are made, they may not agree with every outcome, but they stop assuming betrayal. Transparency converts suspicion into comprehension. That is how trust regrows.

Accountability Is the Bridge Material

Trust cannot survive without accountability. And accountability is not punishment. It is honest feedback, correction without humiliation, repair without denial, and follow-through without delay.
Accountability gaps cause quiet decay long before collapse is visible. People disengage. Energy leaks. Cynicism grows. Accountability is the material that keeps the bridge standing.

Why Trust Must Be Rebuilt Collectively

One-on-one trust is fragile. Collective trust is durable. When trust depends on personalities, it collapses when personalities clash or leave. When trust is embedded in design, it outlasts individuals.
Collective trust rests on shared norms, common standards, mutual protection, and repeatable processes. This is how trust becomes infrastructure instead of emotion.

What Repaired Trust Enables

When trust is restored, capacity returns. Collaboration becomes efficient instead of exhausting. Conflict becomes productive instead of destructive. Leadership distributes instead of concentrating. Growth accelerates without burning people out.
Trust is not emotional comfort. It is operational power.

Why This Chapter Sits Here

Trust could not be addressed earlier. Not before identity stabilized. Not before ownership was named. Not before the division was exposed. Without trust, money becomes isolation. Ownership becomes lonely. Leadership becomes unsustainable. With trust, growth becomes scalable, communities stabilize, and legacy becomes possible.

The Quiet Truth

Most people do not fear cooperation. They fear exposure without protection. Trust repairs that fear, not through words, not through promises, but through design.

Where This Leaves Us

We now understand why division weakened us, why isolation felt safer, why trust broke, and how trust is rebuilt. The next step is love, not romance, not sentiment.

Love as infrastructure

Trust creates connection. Love sustains it.
Chapter 15 reframes love not as feeling, but as structure. Care becomes capacity. Commitment becomes protection. This chapter shows how relationships are governed by roles, expectations, and accountability, not sentiment alone.

Chapter 15 – Love as Infrastructure
Why Feelings Fail Without Structure
Love is often described as a feeling.
That description is incomplete.
Feelings fluctuate.
Pressure does not.
Love that exists only in emotion collapses under instability. Love that is intentionally supported endures. This chapter exists to tell a necessary truth without cruelty: if love does not protect, sustain, and reproduce life, it is sentiment, not structure.
That does not mean love was fake.
It means love was forced to survive without support.

When Love Had to Survive Without Stability

For many of us, love did not disappear. It adapted.
It learned how to exist without consistency, without protection, without backup. Love became flexible instead of firm, emotional instead of structural, intense in moments but fragile over time.
Women learned how to love while carrying everything.
Men learned how to provide without feeling trusted or needed.
Children learned how to grow up early and expect less.
This was not because we did not care. It was because stability was rare and pressure was constant.
When people are raised in survival, love stops planning long-term. It focuses on getting through today. Settling feels safer than hoping.
Endurance replaces expectation.
That is how love survives collapse.
But it is not how love thrives.

Why Love Was Reduced to Emotion

Emotion is easy to celebrate. Infrastructure is harder to maintain.
Power benefits when love is framed as private, personal, fleeting, and romantic. That framing removes responsibility.
When love is only a feeling:
- No one is accountable.
- No standards are enforced.
- No continuity is required.

Emotion without structure burns bright and dies fast. What looks like broken love is often love that was never taught how to stand.

What Real Love Actually Looks Like

Real love is not permissive. It is intentional.
It shows up consistently.
It protects what is vulnerable.
It provides what is necessary.
It corrects what will cause harm.
Love plans.
Love prepares.
Love intervenes.
Anything less may feel good briefly, but it collapses under pressure.

Love Protects First

Protection is love's first responsibility.
Love that cannot protect children, elders, families, and futures is not love yet. It is intention without execution.
Protection requires boundaries, standards, enforcement, and courage. Love that avoids conflict cannot guard life.
Harshness is not the issue.
It is care with teeth.

Love Sustains Over Time

Anyone can love in moments. Infrastructure spans decades. Sustainable love builds routines, creates stability, survives fatigue, and outlasts mood. Families, communities, and nations rise or fall on what sustains them, not what they feel. Feelings initiate. Sustainability carries it forward.

Discipline Is an Act of Love

Discipline has been framed as cruelty. That framing is dishonest. Discipline teaches responsibility, creates safety, and preserves dignity. Neglect disguised as kindness destroys more than correction ever will.
Love without discipline is abandonment dressed as compassion.
The aim is protection, not retribution.
It is practice.

Love Must Reproduce Itself

Infrastructure is measured by what continues after you are gone.
Love that reproduces teaches values, passes skills, models behavior, and builds succession.
If love dies with you, it was incomplete.

Legacy is love that plans beyond emotion.

Why Survival Distorted Love

When people live in survival mode, love becomes transactional, not by choice, but by necessity. Conditional. Reactive. Inconsistent. The issue is not incapacity; it is love being forced to function inside scarcity. It is because love was forced to operate inside scarcity.
Scarcity compresses love. Stability expands it.
What looks like hatred between us is often unresolved grief colliding with exhaustion. Grief shows up as defensiveness. Exhaustion shows up as short tempers. Fear shows up as control. Unhealed disappointment shows up as indifference.
We did not learn to love in peace. We learned about pressure.

A Word to the Single Mother Who Settled

Many women did not choose to raise children alone because they wanted isolation. They adapted because reliability disappeared, support was inconsistent, and waiting felt unsafe. Strength became necessary. Settling became rational.
But strength under pressure is not the same as strength inside structure. Love was never meant to operate alone. Naming that difference is recognition, not accusation.

A Word to the Man Who Learned to Guard Himself

Many men did not withdraw because they lacked love. They withdrew because love felt unsafe. When their contributions went unnoticed. When sacrifice was expected but not honored. When vulnerability was met with judgment instead of care.
So, protection turned inward. Silence replaced honesty. Distance felt safer than disappointment. That is not the absence of love. It is love protecting itself without tools.

Why This Chapter Matters Now

We have named trauma. Rebuilt trust. Clarified ownership. Restored capacity. Without love as infrastructure, none of it lasts.
Trust without love becomes transactional. Ownership without love becomes extractive. Leadership without love becomes domination.

The Quiet Shift

When love becomes infrastructure, families stabilize. Children feel safe. Elders are honored. Conflict becomes repairable.
Love stops being a feeling people chase. It becomes a system people rely on.

Reader Tools: Explore Further

If this chapter surfaced pain, questions, or recognition you were not expecting, additional culturally grounded support is available through the QR code linked below. These resources focus on emotional wellness, relationships, family stability, healing from trauma, and rebuilding trust within Black communities.
They are not replacements for faith or personal responsibility. They exist to support clarity, healing, and restoration where needed.

QR Code Verified Link Live

Where This Leaves Us

We now understand why emotion was insufficient, why durability matters, and why love must be intentional.
Clarity can feel heavy before it feels empowering. Seeing the structure is not the same as being trapped by it.
The next step is discipline.

Not punishment.
Practice.

Mental Freedom, Faith & the Discipline of Healing

Love without discipline dissolves.
Chapter 16 integrates belief, thought, and responsibility. Healing is not passive. Faith is not avoidance. Mental freedom requires structure, practice, and consistency.

Chapter 16 – Mental Freedom, Faith & the Discipline of Healing
Why Healing Requires Structure, Not Motivation

I am often asked, "Are you okay?"
My answer is almost always the same.
"I'm good."
And most of the time, I'm not.
That response is not dishonesty.
It's training.
I learned early that Black men are expected to carry weight quietly. That composure is safety. That emotion is liability. That vulnerability is something you ration carefully, if at all.
I was taught, directly and indirectly, that Black men do not sit across from white therapists and explain their wounds. What would they know about a Black man's struggle? What language would they even have for it? How do you explain survival to someone who has never had to carry it? How do you open your chest in a room where misunderstanding can be turned into pathology, where your survival is mislabeled as disorder, and where that label can quietly follow you long after you leave the room?
That belief didn't come from ignorance.
It came from experience, mistrust, and survival.
But the cost of that training is silence without release.
There are moments when I search for a place where I feel safe enough to cry, not defensively, not briefly, but fully, and nothing comes out. Not because the pain isn't there, but because the body has learned to lock it down so completely that even relief feels unsafe.
That is saying something.
Life is heavy. And as a community, we do not provide many places where Black men can set that weight down without consequence. As a man, expressing real emotional pain often feels dangerous, even with the people closest to you.
There are rules you learn without anyone writing them down. Certain emotions are allowed. Others are stored. Vulnerability sounds good in theory. In practice, it is often remembered, reinterpreted, or later framed as a weakness.
So, men learn to ration truth.
Not because they lack depth.
But because they understand consequence.
You stand tall.
You say you're good.
You keep moving.
Even nature understands something we pretend not to.
The male lion, the symbol of dominance, is groomed, rested, and tended to by his pride. Strength does not require isolation. Somewhere along the way, we were taught that it does.

So instead of regulation, we learned suppression.
Instead of healing, we learned containment.
Instead of discipline, we learned endurance.
Endurance without release eventually breaks something.
Mental freedom begins when a man can tell the truth, not loudly, not publicly, but safely, about the weight he carries and how long he has been carrying it alone.
Healing is not crying on command.
It is creating enough internal and external safety that the body no longer has to guard every feeling as a threat.
That takes discipline.
That takes structure.
That takes faith.
And most of all, it takes permission to be human without surrendering strength.

> *"The greatest pursuit in life is the steady drive toward the person you're meant to become, the tomorrow version of you, knowing that true greatness lies in our ability to continually learn and grow."*
> — Terrance McCray Sr.

Mental Freedom Threatens Control

A regulated mind is dangerous to arrangements that profit from reactivity.
A regulated mind questions narratives, tolerates discomfort, delays gratification, and refuses urgency when urgency is manufactured. That kind of mind is difficult to manipulate.
So, distraction is normalized.
Overstimulation becomes culture.
Noise replaces silence.
Urgency replaces reflection.
A distracted mind does not rebel.
It reacts.
Reaction keeps people busy.
Regulation makes them powerful.
Mental freedom is rare because it requires stillness, consistency, and responsibility, all of which threaten arrangements that profit from chaos.

Faith Is Orientation, Not Emotion

Faith is not optimism.
Faith is not motivation.

Faith is not belief without action.
Faith is orientation.
It is the decision to commit to growth before evidence appears. To maintain discipline before reward arrives. To continue repetition when nothing feels different yet.
Faith is what keeps people consistent when motivation disappears.
You do not need shared theology to practice faith. You need commitment to process.
Faith is what allows discipline to survive boredom, discomfort, and doubt.
Without faith, discipline feels like punishment.
Without discipline, faith becomes fantasy.
Together, they create momentum.

Healing Feels Unsafe Because Chaos Was Familiar

Healing feels threatening because it removes survival patterns that once kept you alive.
The nervous system prefers predictability, even when the pattern is harmful.
Known pain feels safer than unknown peace. Familiar stress feels more controllable than unfamiliar calm.
Growth introduces uncertainty, and the body interprets uncertainty as danger.
This is why people abandon healing and say, "It's not for me."
It was working.
Working feels foreign when chaos has been home.

Discipline Is Containment, Not Control

Discipline is not restriction.
It is containment.
Containment creates safety.
Safety allows regulation.
Regulation allows healing.
Without discipline, healing becomes episodic. Emotional breakthroughs rise and fall. Old patterns return under pressure. With discipline, healing becomes predictable.
The body learns when to rest, when to focus, and when to release tension.
Discipline provides the nervous system with evidence that the environment is stable.
Stability is what allows repair.

Willpower Is a Burst. Discipline Is a System.

Willpower fails because it relies on mood.
Discipline succeeds because it removes negotiation.

People burn out trying to heal through willpower instead of structure.
Decision fatigue sabotages consistency. Design removes choice precisely when choice becomes dangerous.
You do not argue with routines.
You follow them.
What feels like restriction is often relief.

Healing Is Repetition, Not Revelation

Insight feels powerful.
Repetition creates change.
Neural pathways strengthen through practice, not understanding. That means choosing the same boundaries daily. Pausing the same way repeatedly. Making the same decisions even when bored.
Healing is boring on purpose.
Boring builds stability.
Stability builds freedom.
If your healing only works when inspired, it is not healing yet.

Calm Is Power Under Control

Mental freedom does not look dramatic.
It looks like emotional regulation, delayed reaction, thoughtful response, and reduced reactivity. A calm mind sees options others miss. It does not rush to defend. It does not confuse urgency with importance.
Calm is not weakness.
It is power under control.

Why This Chapter Matters

Everything built so far depends on this.
An unregulated mind sabotages relationships.
Mismanages power.
Abandons discipline when discomfort appears.
Without mental freedom:
- Trust fractures
- Love collapses
- Ownership becomes reckless
- Leadership burns out

Healing is not self-care.
It is self-governance.

Reader Tools: Commitment Over Convenience

Healing requires consistency, boundaries, structure, and patience. There are no shortcuts that last. Healing is practiced daily, not when convenient, not when inspired, but when committed.

For readers seeking culturally grounded support around emotional regulation, mental wellness, and disciplined healing practices, additional resources are available through the QR code provided here.

Where This Leaves Us

We now understand:
- Why healing feels unsafe
- Why is discipline required
- Why faith sustains consistency

Seeing the structure is not the same as being trapped by it. Structure is how freedom is built.

The next step is self-love.

Not affirmation.

Stewardship.

Reclaiming Self-Love

Discipline without self-respect becomes punishment.
Chapter 17 reframes self-love as stewardship. This chapter dismantles performative healing and replaces it with ownership, boundaries, and long-term care.

Chapter 17 – Reclaiming Self-Love
Why Identity Must Be Owned, Not Borrowed

I've been there.
I know what it feels like to wake up already tired, carrying a weight you cannot fully name, while the idea of self-love feels distant, even insulting.
Somewhere along the way, self-love was reduced to slogans.
Affirmations without action.
Aesthetics without accountability.
Consumption disguised as healing.
That version was never meant to free us.
It shows up as saying "I'm healing" while tolerating the same disrespect, exhaustion, and depletion.
Repeating positive phrases while remaining overextended and unprotected.
Looking peaceful while the body is burned out.
Buying the tools of healing while maintaining the conditions that continue to deplete you.
That version of self-love is popular.
It is marketable.
It is easy to sell.
And it does nothing to change power.
For Black people, self-love was never meant to be comfortable or consumable.
It was dangerous.
It was discouraged.
It was punished.
Loving yourself in a system built to exploit, erase, and extract from you is not a feeling.
It is defiance.
Real self-love is not what you say to yourself in the mirror for thirty seconds.
It is how you treat your body, your time, your mind, and your future over decades.
It is what you tolerate.
It is what you protect.
It is what you refuse to give away cheaply.
Self-love is ownership.
Ownership of your body when it has been policed.
Ownership of your mind when it has been programmed.
Ownership of your worth when it has been negotiated down for generations.
We were taught survival, not care.
Endurance, not restoration.
Functioning, not flourishing.
Many of us learned how to push through pain, but never how to stop bleeding.
How to be strong for everyone else while neglecting ourselves.

That is not self-love.
That is conditioning.
This chapter is not about feeling better.
It is about becoming whole.
Not affirmation, but alignment.
Not image, but integrity.
Until self-love becomes a structure instead of a slogan, exhaustion will keep being called strength, and neglect will keep being called sacrifice.
That is not love.
That is survival masquerading as virtue.

Why Self-Love Was Made Superficial

People who love themselves deeply protect their bodies, guard their minds, defend their boundaries, and plan their futures.
That kind of love is disruptive.
So, self-love was repackaged as indulgence, ego, appearance, and temporary confidence.
Shallow love is safe for the system.
Deep love is not.

Self-Love Begins with Identity

You cannot love what you do not know.
Identity answers three questions:
- Who am I?
- What do I stand for?
- What do I refuse?
- When identity is unclear, self-love becomes conditional.

Validation replaces authority.
Approval replaces truth.

Why Neglect Was Normalized

Neglect was praised as strength.
Endurance without care became admirable.
Sacrifice without replenishment became expected.
Resilience without repair became identity.
People learned to survive rather than to steward themselves.
Self-love reverses that conditioning.

Why Self-Love Became an Obstacle

Black survival was never built around self-preservation.

It was built around self-suppression.
Safety depended on minimizing needs, rest, and boundaries.
Being useful mattered more than being whole.
Being tolerated mattered more than being protected.
In that context, self-love was never neutral.
It was disruptive.
A Black person who truly values themselves accepts less exploitation, withdraws energy from spaces that demand constant sacrifice, and stops proving worth through suffering.
That kind of person is harder to control.
So self-neglect was rewarded and reframed as virtue.
Exhaustion became commitment.
Overextension became loyalty.
Burnout became responsibility.
Self-love was allowed only as long as it stayed shallow.
Confidence without boundaries.
Comfort without change.
Deep self-love interferes with extraction.
It also carries an internal cost.
When people are trained to survive by overgiving, self-love can feel selfish.
It can feel like betrayal.
Reclaiming self-love requires grieving the version of strength that kept you alive but can no longer carry you forward.

When Self-Neglect Was Called Virtue

Self-denial became righteousness.
Self-sacrifice became love.
Suffering without complaint became character.
Rest was labeled laziness.
Boundaries were labeled selfishness.
Anger was labeled immaturity.
Self-prioritization was labeled betrayal.
For Black men, this often sounded like manhood.
Be hard.
Be silent.
Be reliable under pressure.
Choosing care now is not softness.
It is refusal to be disposable.
If choosing yourself feels wrong, that guilt is not intuition.
It is inheritance.

When the World Still Disappoints You

Self-love does not guarantee fairness.
You can love yourself deeply and still be overlooked.
You can set boundaries and still be mistreated.
You can do the work and still face injustice.
Self-love is not a contract with the world.
It is a contract with yourself.
It is the refusal to let how the world treats you decide who you become.
Your worth is not erased by rejection.
Your dignity is not undone by loss.
Your identity is not determined by unfairness.
Self-love is how you carry disappointment without turning it inward.
It is a practiced response, not positive thinking.
It is sovereignty.

Self-Love Is Stewardship

To steward something is to protect it, maintain it, and prepare it for the future.
Self-love is treating your body, mind, time, and energy as assets, not expendables.
Boundaries are not rejection.
They are clarity.
The body is not an obstacle.
It is a record.
The mind does not need motivation.
It needs hygiene.
Self-love is not comfort.
It is consistency.
Sleep over scrolling.
Preparation over panic.
Boundaries over approval.
Discipline is love applied daily.

The Initiation: Leaving Survival Behind

There comes a point where understanding is no longer enough.
Once you see the conditioning, remaining in self-neglect is no longer inherited.
It is chosen.
Initiation begins when you say:
I will no longer measure my worth by endurance.
I will no longer confuse exhaustion with responsibility.
I will no longer call neglect love.

From this point forward, self-love is not admired.
It is enforced.
You may disappoint people who benefited from your depletion.
You may grieve the version of yourself that survived by disappearing.
That grief is not failure.
It is evidence of growth.

What Self-Love Looks Like Under Pressure

Self-love shows up when it is inconvenient.
Saying no without explanation.
Letting people be disappointed.
Choosing rest when guilt argues back.
Small truths.
Repeated daily.
Ownership always feels strange before it feels natural.

Where This Leaves Us

We now understand:
Identity must be owned.
Boundaries are protection.
Discipline is love.
Stewardship creates worth.
The next step is outward power.
Not ego.
Impact.

Building Power Beyond Ownership

Self-mastery is not the finish line.
Broad change does not happen just because individuals feel better.
They shift when healed people move together.
Chapter 18 moves from personal grounding to institutional construction, from reclaimed selves to collective force.

PART 4 — The Seeds: Building Power, Wealth & Leadership

Chapter 18 – Building Power Beyond Ownership
Why Institutions, Not Individuals, Change Conditions

Imagine a world where individual victories do not quietly expire, where ownership does not end in comfort but compounds into force. A world where personal success feeds something larger than the person who achieved it.

Ownership is the beginning.

Power is what happens when ownership connects, scales, and endures.

Many people stop at ownership and wonder why nothing changes. The truth is uncomfortable: individual ownership is easy to ignore. Coordinated ownership is not.

Power does not come from one person winning.

It comes from coordination that keeps winning without asking permission.

Why Ownership Alone Is Not Enough

Ownership provides position. Power determines whether that position matters. You can own a business, property, or brand and remain invisible to the structures that shape access, policy, and outcomes. That invisibility is not accidental. It is permitted.

Established power can manage individuals. It struggles when people organize. A thousand disconnected owners are easy to ignore. A coordinated network is not.

Success Is Personal. Power Is Structural

Success feels good. Power changes conditions.

Success looks like income, comfort, and visibility. It is celebrated precisely because it ends with the individual. When the person stops, the impact stops. Power works differently. Power reshapes access, defines standards, and sets rules that apply whether anyone is paying attention or not.

This is why success is marketed, and power is resisted.

Success flatters the ego.

Power rearranges the environment permanently.

Institutions Are the Container of Power

Individuals inspire. Institutions govern.

Institutions outlive personalities. They preserve memory, enforce standards, and maintain continuity long after founders are gone. This is why every dominant group builds institutions first and celebrates individuals second.

Banks, schools, corporations, trade associations, and legal frameworks are not emotional entities. They are durable ones. Institutions exist to outlast enthusiasm. That durability is the source of their power.

Why Talent Was Encouraged, but Organization Was Discouraged

Talent is unpredictable but containable. Organization is dangerous.
A talented individual can be praised, promoted, isolated, or replaced. An organized group must be negotiated with. That difference explains why we were encouraged to compete instead of collaborating, brand ourselves instead of building systems, and chase visibility instead of governance.
That pattern was not cultural.
It was strategic.
Talent creates moments.
An organization creates authority.
Authority sets the terms.

How Collective Power Was Deliberately Prevented

Collective power did not fail on its own. It was interrupted.
Organizations were underfunded, surveilled, or destabilized. Leadership was targeted. Coalitions were fragmented through scarcity and competition. Long-term coordination was framed as unrealistic or dangerous. Individual success was rewarded. Collective endurance was discouraged.
Over time, people learned to build alone, protect themselves, and exit early. Not because collaboration was impossible, but because continuity was made expensive. That is how ownership remained isolated and power remained out of reach.

Alignment Creates Force

Power does not require agreement.
It requires alignment.
Alignment means shared direction, coordinated timing, and mutual protection. People do not need identical opinions to move powerfully. They need compatible movement. Alignment concentrates effort instead of dispersing it. That concentration becomes force.

The Four Pillars of Durable Power

Power is not accidental. It is engineered.
Capital provides deployable resources. Without it, influence collapses into ideas.

Coordination aligns action. Without it, energy scatters and influence dissolves.
Continuity ensures survival beyond individuals. Without it, gains die with leadership.
Control governs access, rules, and narratives. Without it, ownership remains symbolic.
Remove one pillar and power leaks.
Remove two, and it collapses.
Power is rare, not because people lack passion, but because sustained discipline is harder than desire.

Why Scale Is the Turning Point

Isolated action is ignored. Scale forces response.
Scale changes negotiation power. It attracts political attention. It forces a response. It creates consequences. Scale is not ego. It is survivability.
Without scale, gains are temporary.
With scale, progress stabilizes.

Power Is Quiet on Purpose

Real power is repetitive, procedural, and unglamorous. It lives in bylaws, audits, governance, compliance, and consistency.
Flash attracts attention.
Boredom attracts stability.
Stability is power's preferred disguise.

Power Without Ethics Repeats Harm

Power multiplies what it carries. Without ethics, power extracts, hoards, and corrodes. With ethics, it stabilizes, protects, and reproduces opportunity.
This is why inner repair came first in this book. Unrepaired people with power do not liberate. They repeat damage at scale.

Why This Chapter Comes Now

We could not talk about power before identity was reclaimed, trust was repaired, love was structured, and discipline was practiced. Power amplifies whatever sits beneath it.
Now the foundation can hold weight.

What Building Power Actually Looks Like

Building power is not heroic. It is collective and procedural.
It looks like shared infrastructure instead of isolated wins. Leadership pipelines instead of personality dependence. Institutions that preserve memory, enforce standards, and survive transition.
Power favors longevity over visibility.
It chooses coordination over spotlight.
When endurance replaces ego, power stabilizes quietly.

Where This Leaves Us

We have moved from awareness to literacy, literacy to ownership, and ownership to coordination.
The next step is skill.
Because power without skill becomes fragile and temporary.

Skills for Tomorrow

Power without skill decays. Chapter 19 focuses on preparation, adaptability, relevance, and foresight. Power shifts toward those who anticipate change, not those who chase it.

Chapter 19 – Skills for Tomorrow
How Skill Access Was Systematically Restricted

Most people do not feel irrelevant.
They feel tired.
Tired of doing everything they were told to do and still feeling behind.
Tired of working harder while security feels further away.
Tired of being told to "learn new skills" without anyone explaining which ones actually matter or why the rules keep changing.
Many people sense something is off, but they blame themselves. They assume they missed a memo, chose the wrong path, or failed to adapt fast enough. What they rarely consider is that they were trained for a system that no longer exists.
The goal here is clarity, not blame or nostalgia. What matters is recognizing the shift that already occurred and understanding how access to skills, not intelligence or personal drive, determines who stays relevant when conditions change.
If you have ever looked at your experience, your work ethic, or your loyalty and wondered why it no longer seems to count the way it once did, this chapter is for you. What follows explains why that feeling is not personal failure, but structural change.
Power never disappears.
It relocates.
Every era changes which skills are rewarded and which are discarded. People do not lose relevance because they lack intelligence. They lose relevance because they mastered rules that were quietly replaced.
This chapter exists to clarify a hard truth most people feel but struggle to name.
The future does not reward effort alone.
It rewards adaptability, influence, and coordination.
Skills are not about talent.
They are about survival.

Why Hard Work Is No Longer Enough

Hard work was once a reliable strategy. Show up on time. Follow instructions. Stay loyal. Learn the job. Get promoted.
That contract collapsed.
Many of our parents did everything they were told. They stayed with companies for decades. They sacrificed health and time. They trained replacements. And still watched jobs disappear, pensions shrink, and security evaporate.
Automation replaced routine labor.
Algorithms replaced middle management.
Outsourcing replaced stability.
Platforms replaced employers.

Unleveraged labor became fragile.
Effort without aligned skills became disposable.
The pattern is structural, not emotional.
It is pattern recognition.

Skills Are the New Infrastructure

Skills determine how people interface with power. They decide who negotiates and who accepts, who designs and who executes, who owns processes and who remains trapped inside them.
Degrees certify completion.
Skills create movement.
A degree may open a door once. Skills determine whether you stay inside, move rooms, or build your own structure entirely.
The future belongs to people who can learn, unlearn, and reconfigure faster than conditions change.

The Skills That Separate Control from Compliance

Some skills never go out of demand because they sit upstream of technology. They are not trendy. They are structural.
Strategic thinking allows people to see how parts interact, identify points of influence, and solve causes instead of symptoms.
Communication under pressure moves ideas into action through clear writing, precise speech, and the ability to simplify complexity.
Negotiation aligns interests, determines outcomes, and often matters more than effort ever will.
Financial literacy reveals how money behaves, how incentives work, and who benefits from confusion.
Decision-making under uncertainty separates leaders from reactors, because indecision quietly costs more than most mistakes.
These skills transfer when jobs disappear.
They scale across industries.
They survive disruption.

The Skills Rising as Routine Work Disappears

As automation absorbs repetition, value shifts to what machines cannot replicate.
Pattern recognition allows people to see trends early instead of reacting late.
Creative problem-solving fixes broken processes instead of patching outcomes.
Coordination turns intention into execution and remains the backbone of power.

Ethical judgment governs amplified impact and functions as risk management at scale.
Learning speed determines whether relevance compounds or decays.
Static expertise expires.
Learning velocity compounds.

Why These Skills Were Not Taught

Most people were trained for predictability.
Dominant institutions needed compliance, specialization, and replaceability.
They did not need people who questioned structures, rearranged incentives, or built parallel alternatives.
Education rewarded obedience over adaptability.
Employment rewarded loyalty over influence.
Risk was framed as recklessness instead of a prerequisite for autonomy.
That training produced workers.
It did not produce architects.
That training is now obsolete.

How Skill Access Was Systematically Restricted

Skill scarcity did not emerge naturally.
It was structured.
Training pipelines favored compliance over adaptability. Advanced skills were separated from the communities that needed them most. Information was fragmented, delayed, or hidden behind credentials. Learning was treated as permission-based instead of necessity-based.
People were trained to perform tasks.
They were not trained to redesign the conditions that controlled their outcomes.
Over time, access gaps were mislabeled as ability gaps.
Relevance was controlled without force.

Skills Are Collective, Not Just Personal

Skills not only elevate individuals.
They stabilize communities.
When skills circulate, dependence decreases. Exploitation weakens. Institutions form. A community with shared skills negotiates differently than one with isolated talent.
That is how skills stop being personal assets and become communal infrastructure.

Skill Stacking Is the Advantage

The future does not belong to people who know one thing perfectly. It belongs to those who combine competencies.
Communication plus finance creates negotiators.
Infrastructure-level thinking plus coordination creates operators.
Creativity plus structure creates builders.
Single skills cap value.
Stacked skills multiply it.

Skills Protect Against Disruption

Disruption does not hurt everyone equally.
People with transferable skills, portable knowledge, and strong networks adapt faster. People trained for a single role panic when that role disappears.
Skills turn chaos into opportunity.

Capacity Over Grind

Learning skills is not grinding harder. It is choosing depth over noise, competence over appearance, and longevity over urgency.
The goal is not to chase trends.
It is to build a capacity that survives them.

Why This Chapter Matters

This chapter exists to restore clarity where confusion was profitable. Many people were taught to equate hard work with security and effort with advancement, only to discover that the rules changed without notice.
Chapter 19 explains why that happened.
It shows how skill access, not intelligence, has always determined relevance, and how systems reward adaptability, coordination, and leverage rather than loyalty alone.
This chapter reframes skills as survival infrastructure, not résumé padding.
It teaches readers how to think about learning in a way that outlasts job titles, industries, and economic cycles.
The goal is not to chase trends.
It is to understand positioning, so relevance becomes intentional instead of accidental.

Where This Leaves Us

We now understand how ownership scales into power, how institutions stabilize influence, and how skills protect relevance.

The next battle is narrative.
Because skill without narrative remains invisible.
And power without narrative gets misunderstood.

Protecting the Brand

Skill without narrative control is vulnerable.
Chapter 20 examines how stories shape reality, how media, algorithms, and perception management determine who is believed, amplified, or erased. This chapter teaches defense against distortion.

Chapter 20 – Protecting the Brand
Media, Algorithms & Narrative Control

Power does not move only through money or institutions.
It moves through stories.
Whoever controls the narrative controls what feels normal, possible, dangerous, or inevitable. This chapter exists because no amount of skill, ownership, or coordination survives long if the story about it is controlled by someone else.
Narrative is not decoration.
It is infrastructure.

Why Narrative Is Power

Narratives shape perception before facts are evaluated. They decide who is trusted, who is feared, who is blamed, who is protected, and who is ignored. Once a narrative is established, behavior follows automatically. People vote, spend, comply, resist, or withdraw based on the story they believe they are living inside.
Power does not need to silence truth.
It only needs to frame it.

Media Is Not Neutral

The media is not a mirror.
It is a filter.
What gets amplified, repeated, or buried is shaped by incentives, ownership, and algorithms. Stories that threaten existing power structures are softened, reframed, or dismissed. Stories that reinforce existing hierarchies are normalized and repeated.
That pattern comes from incentives, not conspiracy.
It is economics.
Media platforms monetize attention. Attention flows toward conflict, fear, outrage, and spectacle. Stability does not trend. Chaos does.

How Algorithms Shape Reality

Algorithms do not reflect society.
They train it.
They reward emotion over accuracy, speed over depth, reaction over reflection, and division over clarity. Content that provokes anger spreads faster than content that builds understanding.
Over time, this creates a distorted sense of reality where extremes feel common, and cooperation feels rare. People begin to believe everyone is hostile, progress is impossible, and trust is foolish.

That belief weakens coordination.
And weakened coordination protects power.

Why Black Narratives Are Especially Controlled

Narrative control over Black communities has always been strategic. Fear narratives justify surveillance. Failure narratives justify neglect. Exceptional success narratives isolate progress instead of normalizing it.

When stories focus only on trauma, dysfunction, or celebrity, they erase infrastructure, discipline, and collective competence. This keeps Black achievement looking accidental instead of reproducible.

Branding Is Not Marketing

Branding is not logos, colors, or slogans.
Branding is expectation.
A brand tells the world what to expect before you speak. It sets the frame through which actions are interpreted.
Without intentional branding, others define you. Mistakes are magnified. Success is questioned. Motives are doubted.
With intentional branding, narratives stabilize, trust accumulates, and credibility compounds.
This applies to individuals, businesses, and institutions.

Why Silence Is Not Neutral

Choosing not to define yourself does not create objectivity.
It creates vulnerability.
When you do not tell your story, someone else will and they will tell it in a way that serves their incentives, not yours.
Silence does not avoid conflict.
It concedes narrative ground.

Narrative and Power Must Align

Narrative without power is ignored.
Power without narrative is misunderstood.
Narrative explains why you exist, what you stand for, what you protect, and what you refuse to become. Power enforces those explanations.
When narrative and power align, legitimacy follows.

Protecting the Brand Means Protecting the Frame

Protection is proactive, not reactive.

It means defining values before crises, clarifying standards before accusations, setting boundaries before negotiations, and documenting processes before disputes.
Strong narratives reduce the need for constant defense.
Weak narratives invite endless explanation.

Why Disinformation Works So Well

Disinformation succeeds when trust is low, attention is fragmented, education is uneven, and fear is high.
Its goal is not belief.
It is confusion.
Confused populations do not organize.
They react.

Media Literacy Is Self-Defense

Media literacy is not skepticism of everything.
It is discernment.
It means asking who benefits from this story, what is emphasized, and what is omitted. Literacy restores agency. Without it, narratives become cages.

Narrative Power Is Collective

Narrative control does not come from one voice. It comes from consistent messaging, reinforced language, shared standards, and ecosystems that amplify each other.
Individual visibility fades.
Collective framing endures.

Narrative Infrastructure in Practice

Narrative power requires platforms, networks, and shared visibility. When communities control how businesses, professionals, and institutions are presented, distortion decreases and trust increases.
Visibility becomes intentional instead of accidental.
Narrative infrastructure is how stories scale without being diluted.

Verified Narrative & Media Infrastructure Resources

Explore Black-owned media platforms, narrative ecosystems, and tools designed to shape visibility, perception, and legitimacy.
These resources support:
- Media literacy and narrative discernment

- Coordinated amplification instead of isolated visibility
- Protection against distortion, misframing, and erasure

These tools are not about popularity.
They are about control of framing.
Use them to reinforce collective narratives, sharpen discernment, and ensure what you build is understood on your terms, not filtered through someone else's incentives.

Why This Chapter Comes Now
Skills allow action.
Ownership creates influence over outcomes.
Narrative protects both.
Without narrative control, skill looks threatening, ownership looks suspicious, and coordination looks dangerous. Narrative makes power legible and defensible.

Where This Leaves Us

We now understand how ownership scales, how skills protect relevance, and how narratives shape perception.
What remains is protection.
Because what is built must be guarded.

Guarding the Harvest

Creation is not preservation.
Chapter 21 addresses longevity, protecting what is built from erosion, mismanagement, and external extraction. This chapter is about durability.

Chapter 21 – Guarding the Harvest
Mindset, Financial, and Social Chains

Building is only half the work.
Protection is the other half.
History is filled with movements, businesses, and communities that made progress but failed to keep it. Not because they lacked vision, intelligence, or effort, but because what they built was never protected.
This chapter exists to name a hard truth most people learn too late: anything valuable that is not protected becomes extractable.
The harvest is not just what you build.
It is what you keep, transfer, and sustain.

Why What We Build Gets Taken

Extraction does not require malice.
It only requires access.
When operations are informal, undocumented, or driven by personality instead of process, they become easy to exploit. When ownership is unclear, rules become flexible. When leadership lives in one person, continuity collapses the moment that person steps away.
Most losses do not happen through force.
They happen through neglect.
People assume good intentions will protect what they build. They won't. Arrangements that rely on trust alone survive only when conditions are easy. Pressure exposes weakness, and informal setups fracture the moment stress arrives.

Why Informality Collapses Under Pressure

Informality feels flexible.
It also feels familiar.
But familiarity is not durability.
When decisions live in people instead of processes, accountability becomes personal. Rules shift based on relationships. Authority blurs. When conflict appears, there is no reference point strong enough to hold the structure together.
What felt communal under calm conditions collapses under pressure.
Formal design absorbs impact.
Informality absorbs blame.

Why Institutions Matter More Than Intentions

Good intentions do not scale.
Institutions do.
Institutions preserve memory. They enforce standards. They survive leadership changes and emotional cycles. They exist so progress does not depend on constant supervision or heroic effort. This is why every durable group builds structures that function without charisma, urgency, or constant motivation.
Institutions do not rely on trust alone.
They rely on design.

What It Means to Guard the Harvest

Guarding the harvest is not paranoia.
It is responsibility.
It means clarifying ownership before confusion appears.
Separating personal and organizational assets so emotion cannot contaminate governance.
Defining decision authority so leadership does not drift.
Establishing succession plans so progress does not die with one person.
Creating dispute resolution processes so conflict does not become collapse.
Protection is not reactive.
It is designed before conflict arrives.

Governance Is Stability, Not Control

Governance is often framed as a restriction. In truth, it is preservation. Governance answers the question every system eventually faces: Who decides? How are decisions made? What happens when people disagree? How does leadership transition without chaos? When these questions are unanswered, power leaks. When they are clearly defined, power compounds.
Governance does not slow growth.
It makes growth survivable.

Succession Is the Real Test

Anything that cannot survive transition is fragile.
Succession is not about death. It is about continuity. If progress depends on one person being present, it is not secure. If leadership cannot transfer without instability, the system is incomplete.
Succession planning is not pessimism.
It is proof that the work matters beyond ego.

Law Is a Shield, not a Threat

Law is not just enforcement.
It is defense.
Clear legal structures reduce ambiguity, prevent internal conflict, limit external exploitation, and protect assets across time. Informality invites interpretation. Interpretation invites extraction.
Clarity closes doors that should never have been open.

Access Is Not Control

Access allows participation.
Control determines outcomes.
Guarding the harvest means moving from inclusion to authority, from visibility to protection, and from goodwill to governance.
Without control, gains remain conditional.
With control, progress stabilizes.

Why Culture Alone Is Not Enough

Culture motivates behavior.
Systems preserve it.
Culture without design fades across generations. What is intentionally built carries values forward when memory weakens. Culture inspires. Design sustains.

What Happens When the Harvest Is Guarded

When protection is designed correctly, trust increases and conflict decreases. Capital stays local. Leadership develops predictably. Stability creates confidence, and confidence attracts investment.
Protection does not slow growth.
It makes growth durable.

Stewardship, Not Hoarding

Guarding the harvest requires discernment, not isolation. Stewardship is the discipline of deciding what must be preserved, what can be shared, and what must be defended. It shifts thinking from short-term gain to long-term continuity. While hoarding reacts out of fear, stewardship plans across generations. It measures success not in quarters, but in what endures long after the current moment has passed.

Why This Chapter Comes Near the End

Protection could not be addressed before ownership existed, skills were developed, and narratives were framed. Protection without purpose becomes control. Protection with purpose becomes legacy.

Where This Leaves Us

We have moved from awareness to literacy, literacy to ownership, ownership to power, and power to protection.
The harvest is real now.
And it must be guarded.

The Next Generation

Protection without transfer is failure.
Chapter 22 turns forward. Legacy is not what you leave behind accidentally.
It is what you prepare others to carry intentionally.

PART 5 — The Harvest: Guarding What We Build

Chapter 22 – The Next Generation
Planting Seeds That Outlive You

The future does not arrive on its own.
It is prepared, trained, and protected.
If the next generation inherits confusion, debt, instability, or fear, it is not fate. It is a design failure. Legacy is not what you build for yourself. Legacy is what continues to work when you are no longer present to correct it.

Why the Next Generation Is Always the Target

Power understands something most people avoid confronting: if you shape the children, you control the future without confrontation.
Attention is redirected early. Expectations are lowered quietly. Capacity is delayed subtly. By the time adulthood arrives, limits already feel normal, and ceilings feel earned instead of imposed.
That is why the next generation must be prepared intentionally, not assumed safe.

Inheritance Is More Than Money

Inheritance is often reduced to finances, but money is only one layer. What children truly inherit is belief.
They inherit how possibility is defined.
How authority is perceived.
How responsibility feels.
How systems are understood.
How much instability is tolerated as normal.
Money amplifies whatever mindset it lands in. Discipline compounds. Dysfunction consumes. Without preparation, assets disappear within a generation. The record is clear: this pattern has occurred consistently over time.

What We Hand Down Without Realizing It

Every household transmits something, whether intentional or not.
Silence teaches avoidance.
Chaos teaches anxiety.
Overprotection teaches fragility.
Neglect teaches self-abandonment.
Even survival strategies that once made sense can become limitations when passed forward without revision.
Children do not inherit intentions.
They inherit systems.

Why Education at Home Comes First

Formal education matters.
Home education matters more.
At home, children learn how life actually works. How decisions are made. How conflict is handled. How money is discussed. How time is valued. How discipline functions.
When those lessons are absent, outside institutions step in.
They do not teach ownership.
They teach placement.

Training Capacity, Not Just Ambition

Ambition without capacity creates frustration.
Capacity is what allows ambition to survive disappointment, delay, and pressure. It includes emotional regulation, delayed gratification, follow-through, critical thinking, and self-trust.
These are not personality traits.
They are trained behaviors.
Children raised without structure struggle to create it later, not because they are incapable, but because repetition was missing.

Why Protection Is an Act of Love

Protection is often confused with restriction. In reality, protection provides boundaries, consistency, predictability, and safety for growth.
Without protection, children adapt to chaos instead of building confidence.
Love without structure feels warm.
It does not scale.

Exposure Shapes Expectation

Exposure creates expectation before choice exists.
What children see repeatedly becomes normal. If they only see employment without ownership, consumption without creation, and visibility without control, those patterns feel inevitable.
Intentional exposure expands imagination. Seeing builders, planners, negotiators, entrepreneurs, and institutions makes future pathways feel reachable instead of theoretical.

Where Understanding Begins

Foundational thinking should not wait for adulthood.
Children can understand how money circulates, how rules are created, how incentives shape behavior, and how organizations function. Knowledge builds capacity, not burden.
It is equipping them.
Clarity reduces fear.
Understanding replaces intimidation.

Responsibility Without Pressure

Preparation does not mean pressure.
Children do not need to inherit anxiety about legacy. They need to inherit competence. Responsibility should be introduced gradually, supported consistently, and modeled visibly.
Children believe what they see working, not what they are told to admire.

Why Time Is the Real Asset

The next generation inherits time differently.
Time compounds learning faster than money compounds interest. What is taught early becomes instinct. What is delayed requires repair.
Time is the quiet advantage most people waste.

Where This Leaves Us

Legacy is no longer abstract.
We now understand why what is built must last, why protection makes it durable, and why preparation must come before inheritance. The next generation does not need perfection.
They need clarity.
Structure.
Continuity.

Legacy Engineering

Inheritance without structure collapses.
Chapter 23 brings this work into permanence. Wealth, land, and law are integrated, so what is built cannot be undone easily or taken quietly.

Chapter 23 – Seed to Stronghold, Protect Wealth and Land

Guarding Wealth and Land So They Cannot Be Stolen Again

Wealth does not disappear by accident.
It is removed through a process.
This chapter exists because too many Black families worked, saved, bought property, and still lost everything within one or two generations, not because they were careless or irresponsible, but because legacy was never engineered.
Legacy is not emotion.
It is structure.
You can love your family deeply and still lose everything if love is not backed by law, clarity, and instruction.

Why Assets Alone Were Never Enough

For generations, Black families acquired assets without protection.
Homes were purchased.
Land was held.
Businesses were built.
And then:
- Property was lost through taxes
- Land was divided until it became unusable
- Businesses collapsed during probate
- Heirs fought or were pushed out
- Outsiders stepped in quietly

Assets existed.
Systems did not.
Wealth without structure is temporary. It does not survive grief, conflict, or time.

Probate: Where Black Wealth Goes to Die

Probate is one of the most destructive and misunderstood forces behind Black wealth loss. It is the court-supervised process that determines what happens to your assets after death when no protective structure is in place. Probate is slow, expensive, public, and adversarial by design. During this period, assets are frozen, legal fees accumulate quietly, family tensions intensify, and opportunists pay close attention.
Probate does not protect families.
It exposes them at their most vulnerable moment, when grief is high, and leverage is low.

Time favors those with lawyers, capital, and patience, not families caught unprepared.
The outcome follows the design.
It is documented history.

The Silent Theft of Heirs' Property

One of the least discussed and most devastating forms of Black land loss is heirs' property.
When property passes without a will or trust, ownership fragments across generations, and dozens of heirs may technically own one piece of land.
Any single heir can be pressured, manipulated, or financially forced into selling their share.
That sale can trigger a partition action, allowing the court to order the sale of the entire property, often at below-market value.
Millions of acres of Black-owned land were lost this way.
Not through violence.
Through law.

What a Will Actually Does (and What It Doesn't)

A will is a legal document that states how you want your assets distributed after death. It reflects intention, not protection. What most families are never told is that a will does not shield assets from the system. It hands them directly to it.
A will becomes active only after death, at the exact moment families are grieving, vulnerable, and least prepared to navigate conflict, delay, and legal pressure. In practice, a will often clarifies wishes but does not control outcomes.
Here is the truth most people are never told:
- A will does not avoid probate
- A will becomes public record
- A will can be contested
- A will activates only after delay, fees, and court involvement

A will is better than nothing.
But it is not protection.
For many families, the real issue is not the document. It is the people. Grief turns old wounds into legal battles. Silence becomes suspicion. "Fair" becomes destructive.
The court does not interpret intentions or preserve relationships.
The court does not guess.
It follows procedure.

Why Trusts Change Everything

Trusts are not for the wealthy.
They are for the prepared.
A trust is a legal structure that controls assets before death, during incapacity, and after death, without court interference.

A Real Example: Inheriting a Home Without a Trust

Let's walk through this slowly, because this is where many families get confused and where good intentions often turn into loss.
Imagine your parents bought a home years ago for $120,000. Over time, the neighborhood improved, and values rose. By the time they passed away, the home is worth $395,000.
That increase in value is called appreciation.
Here is the first truth most people never hear:
You are not automatically taxed on that increase just because your parents passed away.
When a parent dies, the IRS generally applies what is called a step-up in basis. In plain language, this means the value of the house is reset to what it was worth at the time of death, not what your parents originally paid for it.
So instead of the tax system treating the home as if it is still worth $120,000, it now treats it as worth $395,000.
Capital gains tax is based on the difference between the value at inheritance and the price at sale, not the original purchase price.

Why $395,000 Often Means No Capital Gains Tax

If you inherit the home at $395,000 and later sell it for $395,000, there is no capital gain. No profit. No tax.
Even if you sell it for slightly more, say $400,000, the gain is only $5,000. For most people, that amount is either very small or partially shielded by federal exclusions, especially if the home becomes your primary residence.
That is why you may hear people say, "There's no tax if it's under $400,000."
What they really mean is this:
As long as the increase after inheritance is small, capital gains taxes are minimal or nonexistent.

The Catch: Taxes Aren't the First Threat. Process Is

Here is where things go wrong for many families.
If your parents did not place the home in a trust, the property usually goes through probate.
During probate:

- The home is frozen
- No one has clear authority
- Bills still exist
- Property taxes still run
- Maintenance still costs money

Now add siblings.

If there are multiple heirs, each one technically owns a share. But unless everyone agrees on timing, repairs, renting, or selling, nothing moves smoothly.

One sibling wants to keep the house.
Another needs cash.
Another stops communicating.
Another lives out of state.
Under pressure, courts often force a sale.
And here is the quiet part most people miss:
The forced sale is what creates the tax problem.
If the house is sold quickly, under pressure, or after legal fees and delays pile up, families often lose equity. If the sale price rises after probate delays, capital gains can suddenly appear, not because the house was inherited, but because the process dragged on.
The inheritance did not cause the tax.
The lack of structure did.

How a Trust Changes the Outcome

Now imagine the same house, same value, same siblings, but your parents placed the home inside a revocable living trust.
Here is what changes:
- The home does not go through probate
- Ownership instructions are already clear
- A trustee is named
- Decisions do not require court permission
- The transfer happens privately and quickly

If the trust says one child manages the property, another receives cash later, or the home must be held for a set period, that instruction is followed.
No court guessing.
No forced sale.
No chaos during grief.
The trust does not eliminate taxes.
It eliminates confusion, which is what usually creates them.

Important State Differences You Must Check

Estate rules are not identical in every state.
Depending on where the property is located:

- Capital gains rules may vary slightly
- Property tax reassessments may occur
- Transfer-on-death deeds may or may not be allowed
- Heirs' property laws differ

Every reader should confirm, for their state:
- How inherited property is taxed
- Whether probate can be bypassed
- How multiple heirs are treated
- Whether reassessment happens at transfer

Hope is not a plan.
Structure is.

The Revocable Living Trust (The Workhorse)

A revocable living trust is one of the most practical and powerful tools for protecting family assets across generations. It functions during life, incapacity, and death without handing control to the courts.

A revocable living trust allows you to:
- Remain in control while alive
- Move assets in and out as circumstances change
- Avoid probate entirely
- Keep family matters private
- Transfer property smoothly
- Protect intent, not just assets

A trust does not take your property from you.
It wraps it in instruction.
You can change it.
You can dissolve it.
You remain the authority.
Trusts remove chaos, not family involvement.

Why Wills Feel Familiar and Trusts Feel Intimidating

Wills feel simple because they are common.
Trusts feel complex because they are unfamiliar.
But complexity is often just unfamiliar protection:
- Wills invite courts
- Trusts bypass them
- Wills invite conflict
- Trusts create clarity
- Wills ask for fairness
- Trusts enforce stewardship

Wills rely on interpretation.
Trusts rely on instruction.

What feels easier now often becomes more expensive, public, and damaging later.

Bank Accounts, Cash, and the Myth of "It'll Be Fine"

Probate is not only about houses.
Checking and savings accounts can be frozen.
Joint accounts are not always protection.
Improper titling creates access delays.
Tools that can bypass probate include:
- Payable-on-Death (POD) designations
- Transfer-on-Death (TOD) registrations
- Proper beneficiary designations

Money does not disappear at death.
Access does.

Who Inherits Matters Less Than How

Many families focus on fairness.
Equal distribution feels just.
It is often destructive.
Legacy engineering asks harder questions:
- Who can steward this asset?
- Who should control decisions?
- How will conflict be resolved?
- What happens if someone fails?

Legacy is not about equality.
It is about continuity.

Why Education Must Accompany Inheritance

Money without understanding creates pressure.
Heirs who inherit without preparation often:
- Spend defensively
- Avoid responsibility
- Liquidate too early

What looks like entitlement is usually untrained responsibility.
Inheritance without literacy collapses.

Law Can Be a Weapon or a Shield

Law removed Black wealth.
Law can now protect it.
When used intentionally, the law:

- Prevents extraction
- Stabilizes transfer
- Preserves autonomy
- Defends intent

The same system that took can now shield, but only with knowledge.

Reader Tools: Legacy, Land, and Legal Protection

A verified QR code follows this chapter, connecting readers to a curated set of Black-owned, culturally grounded educational resources focused on long-term asset protection, intergenerational continuity, and legacy preservation.

These resources guide ownership structures, asset protection, legal navigation, and informed long-term decision-making.
This section is not a substitute for professional counsel.
It is a gateway to knowledge, preparation, and protection.
This is not legal advice.
It is legal empowerment.

Why This Chapter Comes Near the End
Law locks in what already exists.
Without identity, ownership, power, and discipline, law does nothing.
With the foundation in place, the law preserves everything.

Where This Leaves Us

We now understand:
- Why assets were lost
- How probate extracts wealth
- Why wills alone fail families
- How trusts protect continuity
- Why legacy must be engineered

The tools exist.
The knowledge exists.
What remains is execution.

Planting Beyond These Pages

This book was never the destination.
It is a charge.
Seeds only matter if they are planted, protected, and passed forward.
What happens next determines everything.

Conclusion: Planting Beyond These Pages
The Future Is in Your Hands

> 📖 "You will reap a harvest if you do not give up."
> — Galatians 6:9

The seeds you sow in faith will produce what discipline protects, and love sustains.

This Book Is Not the Harvest, You Are

We have:
- Named the weeds
- Exposed the root systems of oppression
- Reclaimed our soil
- Protected our harvest
- Built strategies that outlive us

But a book does not change generations.
Action does.
A seed only becomes a forest if planted.
If watered.
If protected until it grows strong enough to shade others.

Your Covenant with the Soil

From this moment forward, every choice plants something:
- Speak life into a child
- Heal your mind and protect your body
- Buy land and build systems
- Document your instructions and protect your legacy
- Choose truth over silence
- Choose unity over ego
- Choose faith over fear

Everything is a seed.
And seeds do not stay seeds for long.
They either *grow or rot based* on what you do next.

Manifesto of Seeds

Write this. Say this. Live this:
- I will not leave weeds as an inheritance
- I will plant wisdom, wealth, and story
- I will protect my community's soil from poverty and neglect
- I will pass down ownership, literacy, and love

- I will teach my children to water the seeds I plant so they can plant theirs

This is the revolution:
- Not one leader
- Not one march
- Not one election
- Not one book

But millions of quiet seeds are becoming forests.

The Harvest Vision

Imagine it:
- Families with trust funds and trust in each other
- Communities with gardens, co-ops, schools, and banks we own
- Children who know their story, their worth, their brilliance
- A culture so rooted that no system can uproot it

That is the vision.
That is the future we build by hand, by discipline, and by love.
UPROOT is no longer just a framework on paper.
It is your daily covenant with the soil:
- Understand the Soil
- Protect the Roots
- Remove the Weeds
- Own Our Growth
- Organize Our Garden
- Thrive and Teach

Carry it beyond these pages.
Plant it daily.
Pass it forward.

Ritual Blessing

Place your hand over your heart and speak:
"The soil remembers, and the soil heals.
I plant boldly.
I plant wisely.
I plant in love.
And I watch freedom grow.
My legacy is rooted.
My people are rising.
The harvest begins now.
Ashe. Amen."

The UPROOT Covenant
Seeds over Weeds: A Reader's Manifesto
A Daily Commitment to Plant What Outlives You

> 📖 "Those who sow with tears will reap with joy."
> — Psalm 126:5

The work may feel heavy now, but the harvest will be worth generations of celebration.

Understand This

Every choice I make is a planting.
I refuse to water weeds:
- Poverty
- Division
- Fear
- Betrayal
- Neglect

I choose to plant seeds of:
- Wealth
- Wisdom
- Unity
- Faith
- Love

My Commitments

To Myself
I will uproot lies, fear, and self-doubt.
I will plant discipline, knowledge, and self-love daily.
I will guard my mind as the first land I own.

To My Family
I will not pass down struggle without a strategy.
I will plant financial literacy, ownership, and legacy planning, so my children never start from zero again.

To My Community
I will not feed gossip or sabotage.
I will plant trust, collaboration, and systems that protect us all.

To My Legacy
I will document everything that matters:
wills, trusts, passwords, deeds, family stories, and names.
I will plant wealth and culture as an inheritance for generations.

My Declaration

Place your hand over your heart and speak aloud:
"I am soil.
I am seed.
I am a farmer.
I am harvest.
The revolution lives in me
and it will not die with me."
Ashe. Amen.
Sign Your Covenant
Name: _____
Date: _____
Witness (Optional): _____

Final Step

A covenant is only real if it's repeated.
📌 Post a photo of your signed covenant, where you will see it every day (bathroom mirror, fridge, office wall) It becomes a reminder that: *Every day is planting day.*

Acknowledgments

This book carries my name on the cover, but the truth is, a village wrote it.
To the season that became the soil of this book: when everything else felt unsteady, that season gave me ground to stand on. It reminded me that broken does not mean barren, that even damaged soil can grow a new harvest. Healing did not arrive loudly, but steadily. Hope took root where weeds once dominated, and something honest began to grow in me. Not every season is meant to be permanent. Some exist to prepare us. What mattered was not how long it lasted, but what it produced. For that growth, Osceola, I am grateful.
To my daughters, Faith and Jordyn: you are the roots and the future. Everything in these pages is a promise to you. You are my why, my daily reminder that the story must be better for the next generation. The long conversations, the laughter, the eye rolls, and the "Dad, here he goes again" moments shaped these pages more than you know. You made me want to be better, think deeper, and fight harder for a future worth handing you.
To my grandmother, Laura: you are the root beneath roots. Long before I had language for resilience, I watched it live through you. What you endured, what you protected, and what you carried without complaint shaped generations that followed. Your strength did not announce itself; it sustained us. This book grows from soil you never got credit for tending.
To my mother, Peggy, and my Aunt Charlotte: you carried weight that was never meant to rest on one set of shoulders, yet you did it anyway, with love, discipline, humor, and faith. What you poured into family when resources were thin became the foundation I stand on now. If this book speaks of restoration, it is because you modeled endurance long before I understood it.
To my brothers and sisters: we came from the same soil. We learned early how to survive, how to adapt, and how to keep moving when answers were scarce. Every shared memory, the scars, the laughter, the lessons, shaped the lens through which I see the world. This book carries pieces of all of us.
To those who pushed me with truth and discipline when comfort would have been easier, friends and mentors who demanded clarity, rigor, and responsibility, your insistence on excellence became part of the backbone of this work.
And to the reader: thank you. You chose to pick up this book, sit with it, and walk through these pages. If it does more than inform you, if it stirs you, challenges you, and calls you higher, then it has done its job. Carry the seeds forward. Teach the next. Build the legacy.
Ashe. Amen.
— Ronald Jones

I believe that when you stop learning, you die, mentally, spiritually, and physically. Knowledge is at its best when it is shared, and growth is at its best when that knowledge is applied.

While we must learn from our past and acknowledge what has transpired, we must also turn our gaze toward the future, where we still hold the power to shape our own path. I am thankful to God for granting me the opportunity to offer readers of this book a space to confront deep fears, reflect on past missteps, and embrace the possibility of transformation.

I want to thank my mother, Peggy, for her dedicated support and teachings. To my spiritual father, Elder David Spain, Jr., and my spiritual mother, Church Mother Francis Harper, thank you for pushing me forward and never giving up on me.

One plants, one waters, and God gives the increase.

— Latoya Jones Frazier

About the Authors

Ronald D. Jones Jr. is a retired U.S. Navy Lieutenant Commander, real estate investor, author, and visionary entrepreneur committed to helping people break cycles, build wealth, and create generational impact.
After more than thirty years of decorated military service, where he led teams, trained future leaders, and operated with precision under pressure, Ron carried that same discipline and resilience into the world of business and publishing.
As the founder of Jones Innovative Reality and Jones Innovative Publishing, Ron equips both new and seasoned investors with proven strategies for financial freedom, scalable business systems, and the mindset required to win in today's competitive market. His approach blends hard-earned real estate expertise, tax-smart financial planning, and CEO-level leadership into a practical framework designed to help others move beyond survival mode and into sustainable abundance.
Beyond business, Ron is one of the founders of *Fishing for Fighters*, a nonprofit dedicated to serving active-duty service members and veterans battling PTSD through the healing power of fishing and the outdoors. His work reflects a deep commitment to service, legacy, and giving back, values forged in the Navy and carried forward into every venture.
A passionate writer and coach, Ron's mission is to plant seeds of knowledge that outlive him, empowering readers, investors, and families to create generational wealth and freedom. When he's not writing, mentoring, or negotiating real estate deals, he can be found chasing the sunrise with a fishing rod in hand or spending time with his daughters, Faith and Jordyn.

Latoya L. Jones-Frazier is a dynamic leader, author, and advocate whose life's work sits at the intersection of compassion, action, and transformation.
As the founder and Chair of the Board of Wilcome Human Services, Inc., she has dedicated more than fifteen years to empowering youth and young adults with the tools to rise above systemic barriers. Her organization is more than a nonprofit, it is a lifeline of mentorship, education, and holistic support that helps young people turn adversity into strength and vision.
Her leadership is guided by integrity, rooted in lived experience, and sharpened through professional expertise. She is known for cultivating programs that prioritize resilience, trust, and healing, values she believes are not optional but essential for lasting transformation.
Latoya's passion for storytelling has also made her a published author, with books for children and young adults that remind readers of a simple but profound truth: Their voices matter. In *Seeds in the Soil*, she channels that same conviction into a call for growth, unity, and the reclamation of legacy.

Her impact has not gone unnoticed. Johns Hopkins Medicine honored her with the Martin Luther King Jr. Community Service Award for her unwavering dedication to service, equity, and justice.

Above all, Latoya remains committed to planting seeds of empowerment, growth, and healing that will bear fruit for generations to come.

Notes & References

📖 *Seeds in the Soil — Receipts & Sources*
This book was written to be lived, not debated. Still, truth deserves receipts. What follows are the studies, reports, historical records, and cultural sources referenced throughout *Seeds in the Soil*. They are provided for readers who wish to verify claims, trace systems, and deepen understanding.
This is not an exhaustive academic bibliography.
It is a roadmap.
These sources inform the systems described in this book. They are not quoted exhaustively, but they ground the patterns examined.

Economics, Wealth & Finance
TIAA Institute & Global Financial Literacy Excellence Center (GFLEC). *2025 Personal Finance Index (P-Fin Index).* April 2025.
U.S. Government Accountability Office (GAO). *Retirement Security: Wealth and Savings by Race, 2019–2022.* GAO-23-105941, 2023.
Economic Policy Institute (EPI). *The State of American Wages 2024.* Washington, DC, 2024.
Pew Research Center. *Racial Wealth Gaps in the United States.* Washington, DC, 2023.
Ray, Rashawn; Andre Perry; David Harshbarger. *The Devaluation of Assets in Black Neighborhoods.* Brookings Institution, 2021.
U.S. Department of the Treasury. *Homeownership Rates by Race and Ethnicity.* 2022.
AARP Public Policy Institute. *Access to Workplace Retirement Plans by Race and Ethnicity.* 2022.
National Academy of Social Insurance (NASI). *Social Security and the Racial Retirement Gap.* 2024.
Federal Reserve Board. *Survey of Consumer Finances.* 2022.
NielsenIQ / Selig Center. *The Multicultural Economy 2025.* University of Georgia, 2025.

Civics, Education & Culture
Ramsey, Guthrie P. *Race Music: Black Cultures from Bebop to Hip-Hop.* University of California Press, 2003.
USC Annenberg Inclusion Initiative. *Inclusion in the Recording Studio: Gender, Race, and the Music Industry.* 2024.
Zuboff, Shoshana. *The Age of Surveillance Capitalism.* PublicAffairs, 2019.
Baptist, Edward E. *The Half Has Never Been Told.* Basic Books, 2014.
Pew Research Center. *Social Media Usage Patterns by Race and Ethnicity.* 2024.
U.S. Census Bureau. *Household Broadband Access Report.* 2023.
U.S. Census Bureau. *Voting and Registration Data.* 2024.
Brennan Center for Justice. *Voting Laws Roundup.* 2025.
PEN America. *Book Bans Across America: 2023–2024.*

U.S. Department of Education, Office for Civil Rights. *Civil Rights Data Collection: School Discipline.* 2022.
USC Annenberg Media, Diversity & Social Change Initiative. *Race and Representation in Film and Television.* 2024.
Williams, Heather A. *Self-Taught: African American Education in Slavery and Freedom.* UNC Press, 2007.
Economic Policy Institute. *The Class of 2024: Wages, Debt, and Race in Higher Education.*

Health, Environment & Justice
Centers for Disease Control and Prevention (CDC). *Health Disparities Report.* 2023.
U.S. Department of Agriculture (USDA). *Food Access Research Atlas.* 2024.
Harvard C-CHANGE / EPA / PNAS. *Racial Disparities in Air Pollution Exposure.* 2019–2023.
U.S. Department of Housing and Urban Development (HUD). *Lead-Based Paint Hazard Reports.* 2023.
CDC / NIH. *Asthma Disparities by ZIP Code.* 2024.
Nature Climate Change. "Redlined Heat Islands and Environmental Inequality." 2020–2023.
The Sentencing Project. *State of Incarceration in America.* 2025.
ProPublica. *Heirs' Property and the Racial Wealth Gap.* 2024.

Family, Policy & Social Systems
U.S. Department of Health and Human Services (HHS). *Welfare Rules Database Summary.* 2023.
U.S. Census Bureau. *America's Families and Living Arrangements.* 2023.
Pew Research Center. *Decline of Marriage and Rise of Single Parenthood.* 2024.
Bureau of Justice Statistics (BJS). *Prisoners in 2023.* DOJ, 2024.
GAO. *Child Support Enforcement: Federal and State Roles.* GAO-23-119831, 2023.
McLanahan, Sara; Garfinkel, Irwin. *Fragile Families and Child Wellbeing Study.* Princeton University, 2022.
Coates, Ta-Nehisi. "The Black Family in the Age of Mass Incarceration." *The Atlantic,* 2015.
Bandura, Albert. *Social Learning Theory.* Prentice Hall, 1977.

Technology, Media & Digital Power
NielsenIQ. *Digital Economy Report.* 2024.
MIT Media Lab. *Gender Shades.* 2018.
National Institute of Standards and Technology (NIST). *Face Recognition Vendor Test: Demographic Effects.* 2023.
Harvard Kennedy School, Shorenstein Center. *Social Media and Emotional Contagion.* 2023.
NAACP & Brookings Institution. *The Black Digital Divide Report.* 2024.
White House Office of Science and Technology Policy. *Blueprint for an AI Bill of Rights.* 2022.

Pew Research Center. *AI and Public Trust Survey.* 2025.

Legacy, Land & Ownership

USDA / Federation of Southern Cooperatives. *Black Farmland Loss Since 1910.*

McKinsey & Company. *Race in the Workplace.* 2021.

Fortune Magazine. CEO Demographics Reports, 2020–2025.

Axios. Fortune 500 Black CEO Reporting.

Business Insider. Fortune 500 Leadership Demographics.

National Funeral Directors Association (NFDA). *Funeral Cost Survey.* 2024.

Caring.com. *Estate Planning and Wills Survey.* 2024.

American Express. *State of Women-Owned Businesses.*

Harlem Capital / HBR / Crunchbase. *Black Founders and Venture Funding Reports.*

History, Culture & Legacy Anchors

Madigan, Tim. *The Burning: Tulsa 1921.*

Oklahoma Commission Report on the Tulsa Race Massacre.

D'Orso, Michael. *Like Judgment Day: Rosewood.*

Kersten, Andrew E. *A. Philip Randolph.*

McGhee, Heather. *The Sum of Us.* 2021.

Plato. *The Republic,* Book VII.

U.S. National Archives. *Fannie Lou Hamer Testimony,* 1964.

Garvey, Marcus. *Philosophy and Opinions of Marcus Garvey.*

Woodson, Carter G. *The Mis-Education of the Negro.*

Biblical & Cultural Sources

Scripture quotations are taken from the Holy Bible unless otherwise noted. (Proverbs 4:23; Proverbs 13:22; Proverbs 18:21; Proverbs 22:28; Psalm 24:1; Psalm 78:6–7; Psalm 133:1; Romans 12:2; Galatians 5:1; Galatians 6:9.)

African Proverbs:

"When spider webs unite, they can tie up a lion."

"Until the lion learns to write, every story will glorify the hunter."

"The child who is not embraced by the village will burn it down to feel its warmth."

"When there is no enemy within, the enemies outside cannot harm you."

Author's Note

These sources were not gathered to impress scholars.

They were gathered to arm our people with receipts.

Evidence that systems were designed.

Proof that survival was never weakness.

And direction for rebuilding what was taken.

www.ingramcontent.com/pod-product-compliance
Lightning Source LLC
Chambersburg PA
CBHW070636030426
42337CB00020B/4031